Missing Peace

Missing Peace

A Modern Parable on
Recovering Your Soul
in a Material World

Glandion Carney

PageMill Press
A Division of Circulus
 Publishing Group, Inc.
Berkeley, California

Missing Peace: A Modern Parable on Recovering Your Soul in a Material World

Copyright © 2001 by Glandion Carney
Cover Photos: Skyscrapers-Karen Beard/STONE
 Hands in Prayer-Colin Hawkins/STONE

All Rights Reserved under International and Pan-American Copyright Conventions. Published in the United States by Wildcat Canyon Press, a division of Circulus Publishing Group, Inc. No part of this book may be reproduced in whole or in part without written permission from the publisher, except by a reviewer who may quote brief passages in a review; nor may any part of this book be reproduced, stored in a retrieval system, or transmitted in any form or by any means electronic, mechanical, photocopying, recording, or other, without written permission from the publisher.

Publisher: Tamara Traeder
Editorial Director: Roy M. Carlisle
Marketing Director: Carol Brown
Art Director: Leyza Yardley
Production Coordinator: Larissa Berry
Copyeditor: Dorian Gossy
Proofreader: Shirley Coe
Cover Design: Jeff Wincapaw
Interior Design: ID Graphics
Typesetting: A Page Turner

Typographic Specifications: Text in Goudy 10.5/15, headings in Gillsans.
Printed in the United States of America

Cataloging-in-Publication Data
Carney, Glandion.
    Missing peace: a modern parable on recovering your soul in a material world/ Glandion Carney.
      p. cm.
    ISBN 1-879290-18-9
      1. Women—Fiction. I. Title.
PS3603.A76 M5 2001
813'.54—dc21

2001034608

Distributed to the trade by FaithWorks, a division of National Book Network
10 9 8 7 6 5 4 3 2 1   01 02 03 04 05

Contents

An Editor's Note vi
Acknowledgments vii
1 / Self-Encounter 1
2 / Conversation 7
3 / Rhythm, Harmony, and Balance 17
4 / Twelve Notions 23
5 / An Old Monk 35
6 / Invitation 47
7 / A Wakening 63
8 / Crisis 67
9 / Conflict 73
10 / Monday: Transition 81
11 / Tuesday: Change 95
12 / Wednesday: Seven Smooth Stones 109
13 / Thursday: Regret and Forgiveness 119
14 / Friday: Prayer 133
15 / Saturday: Good-Bye 145
16 / Letters 157
Epilogue 173
Works Cited 177
About the Author 179
About the Press 180

An Editor's Note

Dear Reader,

What you have in your hands is not a novel. Although it is a story. A story with the elements of parable (a narrative that teaches a lesson) and some elements of allegory (a contrived setting which makes sense in itself but is also meant to signify a second order of reality). But most importantly, this is a story that *teaches*, as all good stories do in some one way or other.

So this is not a story with a complicated plot or finely tuned characterizations; it is a simple story about modern life and the incredible struggle that all of us have to find meaning and purpose in life. It is a story about how people help each other and how we can learn from each other. In this sense it is a story that might be told in any setting and in any group. And it is a story about how spiritual reality reveals its presence in the lives of ordinary people.

Stories that teach us about God and spiritual life have a long tradition, from very early religious and mythic texts to the Bible to modern storytellers, teachers, and preachers. All of those stories can help us understand our own individual story in some particular way. If we choose to participate in those larger stories in ways suited to our own individual needs and wants, it can expand our spiritual understanding. Eventually we each will tell our own story by the life that we live. I hope you will enjoy this story as much as you should be enjoying your own.

Roy M. Carlisle
Editorial Director
PageMill Press

To Kathy & Kelly Orr
A deeply committed Christian couple
Dedicated to the development of
Spiritual formation in all who follow Christ.

Acknowledgments

In the development of Missing Peace, I had several partners who contributed to the manuscript and to whom I am very grateful.

Ginni Freshour: Without her help in forming the characters and concepts, there would be no *Missing Peace*. Her skills were invaluable to the completion of this project. Thank You Ginni!

Dr. Kelly Orr: A psychologist whom I met at a Renovare Conference some years ago. We became very close friends. His counsel was used to develop the values and wisdom that were expressed in the character of Brother Theodore.

Richard Parker: Who's love for jazz helped us all see the beauty of rhythm, harmony, and balance in that music.

Dorian Gossy: For her strong developmental skills. She was able to simplify and clarify scenes and dialogue. And Shirley Coe whose proofing and editing skills served to help make this a better book.

The PageMill Press Team: Roy, Tamara, Patsy, Leyza, Larissa, Nenelle, Jennifer: For their diligence and hard work and their care for me as an author, and Carol Brown for her faithful friendship and ongoing encouragement.

The Renovare Team: For their prayers and encouragement to venture into new areas of faith and formation.

And finally, my wife Marion, for her loving support and patience while working on this project.

Chapter 1
Self-Encounter

It was the first Friday night in May. After a long trip from Chicago to northern Wisconsin, and after an even longer, more strenuous week before that, Joan Alexander sat exhausted on the porch of the cabin she had wrested from her ex-husband, Charles, in their divorce settlement. He had left Joan two years ago for another woman, a doctor with whom he worked. A successful Chicago attorney, Joan had weathered the past two years with stoicism and the singular focus that was her greatest strength—the ability to concentrate on her work no matter how unraveled her personal life was. Though Charles and his girlfriend had lived together since, Joan had been unprepared for how hard it would hit her when they finally got married. And their wedding had been tonight.

The cabin had always been her favorite retreat. It felt good to be out of work clothes. She had even left all her work at home for a change. She only had her cell phone, in case her family needed her. Joan's ash-blonde hair, just developing a pleasant silvery sheen, was clasped back in a butterfly clip. Her long, slim legs stretched in front of her were as good as when Charles had married her. She had kept her lean figure through no particular effort. Good genes. But her hair needed a new style, and her blue-green eyes were bloodshot tonight and burned, partly from the drive up and the dry air up here in Wisconsin, partly from tears that she controlled only with the most determined effort.

Two of her colleagues from the law firm were with her. Margaret, tall, also thin, and auburn-haired with hazel eyes, was a high-powered lawyer more driven than Joan, and whose personal life was in even worse shambles than Joan's. She kept her figure through her pack-a-day habit, which had also given her a gravelly voice. Tracy was an efficient, level-headed African-American paralegal whose good humor and quick wit kept the law partners sane. Tracy had been through her own divorce six years earlier. And though she was committed to her work and did it well, she also took good care of her three kids. In addition, everyone knew she was active in her church, though she didn't wear her religion on her sleeve. Joan appreciated that about Tracy, who aspired to being a lawyer herself someday.

This evening, her friends were already in bed, but Joan, still restless, had come out to the porch to wind down. There were no city sounds—no phones, no stereo from her son's room, no cars, no lights. She only heard the noisy crickets, a distant owl, and the stiff spring breeze. Natural, peaceful sounds.

But inside herself there was no peace. Though she could get away from the frenetic city, Joan realized with chagrin that she couldn't get away from herself, from her angry and painful thoughts. Truth be known, she'd rather be by herself. But she couldn't face being alone in this place she had shared with Charles. Not on his wedding night. *This was a really stupid idea. What ever possessed me to come up here this weekend? This is worse than if I'd stayed at home.*

Joan wiped her eyes, rubbed the back of her neck, put her head back on the Adirondack chair, and closed her eyes. Though it was May, it was still cool this far north. The mug of hot apricot tea felt good in her hands, and the liquid warmed her body as she drank it, but it did nothing to reach the chill deep inside that had nothing to do with Fahrenheit or Celsius.

When she was really honest with herself, Joan knew she was just as guilty as Charles for the marriage's dissolution. Though he was the one who had chosen another marriage partner from among his colleagues, she was all too aware that the people closest to her, male and female, were the people she worked with. She had become married to her job.

Now, at forty-eight years old, her two youngest children were in college—Brad at the University of Wisconsin in Madison, and Alison far away in England studying English literature. Her eldest, Chip (his real name was Charles, after his father), had just graduated from college and was living at home to earn money for law school. They'd dreamed of him becoming a doctor like his father. Instead, he had shared her interests in history, politics, and law. And Chip would be at his father's wedding tonight, standing up for him.

Having Chip stay with her did not seem to fill her deep emptiness. *I'm not alone but I'm still so lonely. The kids long ago learned to live without me. My fault of course.* She knew she could excel at only one thing at a time, and her career had been her highest priority. They had put the kids in daycare so they could concentrate on their professions. And where had it left her? *I've not only lost Charles, I've lost my kids. Someone else taught them to walk, taught them to talk, took them to school their first day. Maybe I can do that for my grandkids.* Joan choked on a sob, surprised at the anguish that she felt welling up inside her, at the self-deprecation, the self-hate. *Maybe I can still reach Chip while he lives with me.*

―――

In the cabin on her makeshift cot, Tracy heard Joan's restlessness and her pain escaping in ragged sighs and whispered curses. Margaret, beside Tracy on her own cot, had finally fallen asleep after putting earplugs in her ears. "The crickets are getting to me," she had told Tracy, as if to deflect the fact that they could both hear Joan's anguish.

Why did I come up here? Tracy wondered. She liked working for Joan, but she didn't always like Joan. Tracy had only worked for Joan a couple of years, having come to the firm after Joan's divorce. And though she didn't approve of the firm's gossip mill, it had helped her understand where Joan was coming from. Apparently the divorce had been nasty and a humiliating surprise for Joan. Colleagues had commented that afterward Joan developed a hardness that she hadn't had before. And a mean edge.

Tracy sighed as she heard another curse and shifted on her mattress. She understood some of Joan's pain. From what she could tell, she'd had better support than Joan during her own crisis. But Joan should know that she'd helped to create her own situation through her drivenness and workaholism. Still, Tracy winced at how mortified Joan would be at what they'd heard in the cabin.

―――

Joan pulled her heavy cardigan sweater more tightly around her in the stiffening breeze. When she and Charles had come up to the cabin, three or four times a year and usually without the kids, they had generally worked all day Saturday, then sat out under the stars at night. It was the one way they had allowed themselves to enjoy nature while they'd escaped the claustrophobia of downtown Chicago. After working all day Saturday, they would fix their favorite nightcaps—a White Russian for her and a brandy for him—and sit and gaze at the stars and talk. Those had been their best conversations during the last six or seven years of their marriage. *Maybe if we'd come up more often we'd still be together.* Joan could almost taste her bitterness.

Usually she loved to consider the stars, their distance, their huge numbers, the vastness of the space they inhabited; though she often speculated about how it could all have come to be— there probably was some creator who had started the universe on its way, with a big bang or something, then left it to wind itself down—tonight the stars gave her no pleasure. Instead of enjoying the vastness of the universe, she only felt insignificant and unimportant. Alone. So alone. And if there were a creator, he—or she—had long ago abandoned creation, maybe moved on to other universes. Such a being certainly didn't care about her rotten life.

Tears coursed down her cheeks, drenching her neck, and adding to the evening chill. She sniffed loudly and hugged herself as the wind became sharper and the cold seeped into her bones. Finally, spent by her unexpected misery and the brutal self-analysis, she became overwhelmingly sleepy. She stood up, turned her back on the universe, and went inside to bed.

Chapter 2
Conversation

The next morning the three women lingered over coffee after they had eaten Joan's decadent but delicious breakfast—French toast with real maple syrup and sausage. And plenty of hot coffee. The circles under Joan's eyes were obvious. The other two women had seen them before Joan had tried, unsuccessfully, to obliterate them with makeup.

"And what were you doing under the stars half the night?" Margaret's coffee cup was halfway to her mouth and her steel-blue eyes were fixed on Joan "By the way, this is great coffee. Like my T-shirt says, 'Coffee, chocolate and men—they are all better rich.'"

"You got that right," Tracy grinned.

Joan replied, "Thanks. I'm fussy about coffee so I leave a good coffee maker up here. Bought the beans yesterday."

"Mmm-mmm good," said Tracy. Then turning to Joan, "You okay, Joan?"

Joan recoiled inside. It was outside of professional bounds to talk too much about emotion and personal angst among colleagues.

"I'm fine. Just needed to unwind a bit." She straightened up, trying to look more cheerful.

"Ladies, I'm going for a walk. Anyone want to join me? There are some great trails around here. Excellent time to walk, by the way—not too cold, not too hot." *Like I'm so experienced at walking these trails,* she chided herself.

"I'm on board, as soon as I get my shoes." Tracy moved to the corner of the cabin by her cot where she'd kicked them off the night before. "Say Margaret, I think I know someone who's going to pretend it's just another Saturday and sit in front of the computer all day."

"See, Tracy, you don't really want to become a lawyer," Joan said. "We're all cursed workaholics whose personal lives are in the trash."

Leaving Margaret to her own devices, they walked for a long time in companionable silence. Tracy spoke first. "It sure does feel like spring—balmy, sun on our backs, birds singing away."

"It's been so long since I've even noticed. Charles and I used to come up here about four times a year. We worked our tails off, like Margaret will do today, but at least we got away. After a nice breakfast on Saturday we'd be at our laptops. Usually my mind was so into what I was working on I forgot to notice the seasons or the weather. I don't know how long it's been since I noticed the breeze in my face."

"That's a shame. It's so beautiful here. I could be happy here for a couple of weeks just fixing meals and taking walks and reading and napping. Ooh, that sounds good," Tracy murmured.

"Napping," Joan mused.

"Naps are part of my religion, Joan. Every Sunday I take a nap after church."

Joan looked at Tracy and half-smiled. "Sounds nice. I don't think I've had a nap since my youngest was born. Actually, though, Charles and I usually did take time to sit under the stars after we'd worked all day. We'd cook a nice dinner together and take it outside to eat while the sun set. We'd mix our favorite drinks and sit on the porch for a couple of hours and talk. We had some of our best conversations then." Joan cleared her throat of a rising sob.

"You okay?"

"Yeah, yeah, fine." She swallowed the sob and blinked away the tears. "I guess we should have come up more often."

"Could be." Tracy left it at that.

They walked on. Joan tried to concentrate on the natural sensations confronting her as they walked. The air smelled green, like grass being mowed on still-wet earth. Old leaves crunched; twigs snapped underfoot. Above them the birds twittered and cawed. Tracy giggled as Joan jumped at the squirrel they scared out from under the brush, and they both laughed when a groundhog lumbered across the path ten feet in front of them. Joan began to relax. By one o'clock in the afternoon, they opened the cabin door to the aromas of cornbread and Italian chili greeted them. Margaret sat typing at the table.

"I got hungry so I went ahead and fixed lunch. Figured you'd hear your stomachs growling soon."

Joan realized suddenly that she was, indeed, hungry again. She ladled out a bowlful of chili each for herself and Tracy, and Tracy cut cornbread, still warm from the oven. They moved out onto the porch where the Adirondack chairs beckoned them. Setting their chili on the wide arms of the chairs, they ate slowly, savoring the flavorful food.

"I just may take a nap, lady. The sun feels so nice and warm."

"Sounds good to me, Tracy." Joan took a deep breath, leaned back and closed her eyes, and did just that, her anguish temporarily at bay.

After dinner Joan and Tracy retreated to the porch once again so Margaret could keep working. While watching the sun set, Joan could deny the truth no longer.

"My ex-husband got married last night."

"Girl?" Tracy snapped to attention.

"I thought coming up here would help me get through the weekend, but last night it really got to me."

"I'm so sorry, Joan."

"It's okay. I'm better now. The walk did me good. You're divorced, Tracy. How long did it take you to get over your ex?"

"Well, it's been a while since I thought about it. It was really a gradual process. Every once in a while I'd suddenly realize that I wasn't quite so angry, or wasn't quite so hurt. One day I realized I was actually enjoying my new life. That was a turning point, I guess. But it was slow. It's been six years for me, and it wasn't until a couple of months ago that I felt fully recovered. How long has it been for you?"

"Two years. Seems like long enough to get over a disappointment."

"Depends on the disappointment."

"How do you mean?"

"Well, who walked out on whom, what the reasons were. Reasons have a lot to do with how someone recovers and how long it takes."

"Yeah, you're probably right. Charles left me. And for one of his colleagues at work, another doctor."

"Hmm. Was it a surprise?"

Joan harrumphed. "It was for me. Shows how in touch with him I was."

"You probably felt betrayed."

"Oh, yeah. Betrayed. Pissed on. Shocked. I'm still mad as hell at him for leaving me, for finding someone else when I haven't, for just being so gosh-darn happy." Even as she spoke, even as the anger clenched in her throat, she questioned her openness. *I can't believe I'm sharing this. It's so personal. Will Tracy lose respect for me?*

"I know the feeling, lady," Tracy responded. "I've been there. There are words for what you are probably feeling. Words like anger. Grief. Rage."

Joan snorted lightly. "Those would be good descriptors, all right. Did you feel those things, Tracy?"

"Sure. Those are normal reactions."

"You seem to have come through it."

"Well, first of all, I didn't do it on my own. You know the saying, 'It takes a village to raise a child'? The people at Union Tabernacle are my village. I don't know how I could have coped through my divorce and the last few years if it hadn't been for my church. After Johnson left they brought my family meals three times a week for a month. They stayed with my kids while I looked for a job. But they don't just help me with my kids. They help me cope with the rest of my life."

"That's neat, Tracy."

Joan shifted her eyes from Tracy's face to a distant point. "I wish I had a village. I mean other than the partnership. My 'village' is that workplace. I won't get any meals brought to my house from that village. Of course, I no longer need the babysitters, thank God."

They both laughed.

The pale luminescence of dusk deepened to the velvety blue-blackness of night. The stars began to shine one by one.

"You know, Tracy, being out here sometimes makes me think about how the universe began."

"Mmmm."

"Do you ever think about how it came to be?"

"I do wonder at it all. I believe in a God who did it, but I wonder how He did it. I get caught up in amazement at the majesty of it."

Joan shrugged. "I guess I believe in a higher power of some kind. But I think that that Being spun the universe out then went on his or her way, letting it all wind itself down over the eons."

"I guess we have a different idea about God. I think he still cares about his creatures on this earth."

"It must be comforting to have that kind of faith."

"Without that, I don't know where I would be, Joan. Again, my village, my church. It wouldn't be there if the people didn't share a strong belief in a personal God. And the village encourages my faith."

"Hmm. I guess I'm just not very religious."

"Have you ever been?"

Joan wasn't sure about this conversation. "Not really. We went to church when I was younger, to a Presbyterian church in our neighborhood. But when I was ten, we moved to the North Shore and never really got around to it again. I've only been in church since then for weddings, funerals, and christenings."

"Do you ever think about church?"

"To be honest I don't have much use for organized religion."

"Hmm. What about other kinds of spirituality?"

"What do you mean?"

"Well, did you ever write poetry, get into music, that kind of thing?"

"In high school I liked poetry. I guess I wrote some myself. I really liked literature a lot."

"What about now?"

"Oh, you know how it is with lawyers. We don't have much time for anything but law. Law school actually beat any poetic or literary stuff out of me. You know, study, study, study; get As, win, succeed; analyze, argue, defend."

"Do you like jazz, Joan?"

"Huh? It's okay. A little goes a long ways. I don't really understand it."

"Well, it helps to understand music, any kind of music. Do you ever wonder why they call jazz 'soul music'? It's because it gets way down deep and stirs up the emotions and the soul and the spirit. My favorite collection is one by John Coltrane—his rendition of 'You Don't Know What Love Is' is great—want to borrow it?"

"Sure. I need to broaden my horizons a bit. I could start with a new music genre. Let's set up a time to talk more when I get back to my calendar. But right now I'm afraid I'm going to have to call it a day. I can't keep my eyes open anymore."

Both women yawned in a most unprofessional way. Then giggled. They went quietly into the cabin and found their cots. Tracy was snoring lightly within moments, and Joan faded away soon after.

Joan and Tracy met the next Friday for their weekly appointment in Joan's office to review the past week and look ahead to the next week's schedule. As was their habit, they got work-related issues out of the way first. Most Fridays when they finished talking about work, Joan would ask Tracy about her law classes that week. She would dispense some of her hard-earned wisdom in response to Tracy's issues at school. Since the semester was over, they wouldn't be talking about school for awhile. But after completing business, Joan abruptly took on her mentoring role anyway.

"You know, Tracy, I don't want to scare you, but you need to know that it takes enormous discipline to be a cutting-edge lawyer. And total commitment to the job. It is a tough life for spirituality and for relationships. The rational comes first. The client comes first. Before everything else. Before your family. Before your health. Before your own psychological well-being. And you are always looking for what's wrong in a case, not for what's right. What really stings for me is that being so successful led to the death of my marriage, the death of my person in some ways. So you need to make some hard choices. Do you want to succeed in law or do you want to succeed in life? In the beginning, when you start out, it looks good to succeed in law, it looks glamorous; you have all these ideals about truth, justice, yada, yada. But when you get to my place in life, you begin questioning whether the personal sacrifices are worth it."

Tracy looked at her wide-eyed, her mouth agape in surprise. Joan realized she had come across a bit strong. She lightened up.

"Sorry, but I've been thinking about last weekend's conversations. I didn't mean to be so harsh, but these really are things you need to think about. I know your family, your friends, your 'village' are all important pieces of your life. But if you want to be a cutting-edge lawyer, you need to think about whether you can do that and hold on to the other important things in your life."

There was an awkward pause. Tracy considered her fingers, then looked up. When she spoke it was in a small voice, "Can we talk about this some more some time?" She almost seemed shy. "Continue, you know, that conversation we started at the cabin?"

There wasn't much Joan wouldn't do for her loyal friend and coworker. But something else made Joan feel a tiny eagerness. "I could see you tomorrow—before my usual working Saturday. Ten fifteen? At that new bookstore-coffee shop on Michigan Avenue, what's it called?"

"Oh, the Michigan Avenue Book Café?"

When Tracy raised her eyes to Joan's, they were warm and bright. "I'd like that."

Chapter 3
Rhythm, Harmony, and Balance

Saturday the two women arrived almost simultaneously at the Michigan Avenue Book Café. Both ordered double skinny lattes, Tracy's laced with caramel and Joan's sprinkled lightly with mocha. At just past ten the place was already bustling with people—many in for coffee, others browsing the bookshelves. The close air inside the bookstore intensified the rich aroma of freshly ground gourmet coffee beans.

Joan wore a pale gray silk blouse and matching gray linen trousers. A string of gray baroque pearls hung about her neck, and a pair of stone-colored Birkenstock thongs shod her feet. The silver barrette holding back her hair, silver studs in her ears, thin silver bracelets on her right wrist, and stainless steel watch on the other arm accentuated the monochromatic effect. She knew that she looked elegant, especially for a Saturday morning.

But next to Tracy she felt very plain. Her friend was flaunting her eclectic, artistic personal style. Since yesterday, Tracy's hair had been styled into twists that fell to her shoulders. She had tucked a bright turquoise silk blouse neatly into a straight wrap skirt printed with bold turquoise, yellow, and red flowers and green palm fronds. Tracy's long, slender frame carried the large pattern well, and her beautiful, chestnut-colored skin both enhanced the brightly colored outfit and was enhanced by it. Tracy's earrings of large copper circles fell almost to her shoulders and jangled playfully. Joan noticed people's attention turning, especially to Tracy, as they glided gracefully across the room.

The two women found a small table close to the window and settled themselves. Tracy's earrings swung as she sat down.

"I like your hair, Tracy."

"Thanks. My daughter did it for me."

The women looked at each other and smiled tentatively. Except for the weekend at the cabin, they had never done anything together socially.

"I brought that John Coltrane disc I mentioned to you."

"Great. I'm looking forward to listening to it."

"This is *Ballads*, by the John Coltrane Quartet. Check out 'You Don't Know What Love Is,' like I suggested. I liked John Coltrane the first time I heard him. His melodic kind of playing tells the story of emotions and depth, which makes me appreciate the rhythm and flow of my own life."

"Rhythm, huh?"

"Yeah. Rhythm, harmony, and balance. They're important in our lives just like they are important in music."

"Say more about that, Tracy." Joan was peering into Tracy's eyes, chin in her hand, elbow on the table

"Well, I guess rhythm is letting your inner core values set the pace for your life."

Joan frowned in concentration.

"Here is what I mean," Tracy continued. "I spend time every day just being quiet. For ten minutes after the kids have left for school, I just sit quietly and try to be aware that God is with me; I try to listen to what he might be saying to me inside.

That's part of my daily rhythm. My weekly rhythm includes church on Sunday and that nap I mentioned at the cabin." She gazed out the window for a moment, then looked back at Joan.

"You know, it occurs to me just now that for me, coming to work every day and going to law school classes two evenings a week are part of my rhythm, too, because I'm doing them out of one of my core values—the value of giving my life to helping people. I hadn't thought of that before." Tracy stilled the sway of an earring with her long fingers and looked into space, smiling, as though pleased with the idea.

"That's cool, Tracy. So for you the study of law isn't something you're using to get ahead in your own life. It's truly part of who you are inside."

"Yeah. There's harmony in it all, see?" Tracy said. "The harmony and rhythm overlap each other. Harmony is living in a way that validates your core values so your life is lived with purpose. If something is a value for you, you either incorporate it into your life or you don't feel right.

"Say you value nature. It's spring, and the flowering crab apple trees along the boulevard are at their peak. When you let that beauty nourish you, that's living in harmony with your value of nature."

Joan nodded, letting Tracy know she understood.

"Or say it's really important to you to treat all people with dignity. If you are living in harmony with that value, you will acknowledge even the janitor at work, or the homeless person on the street. You'll treat your coworkers and clients alike, with respect and dignity. That's living in harmony."

Tracy sat up to her full height, her florid gestures making the men at the next table smile. "Of course, people will achieve rhythm and harmony in different ways. During the week maybe they are real focused, or their particular job prohibits them from enjoying nature—it's in a dark place without windows, for example. Then they have to schedule nature into their time off."

Joan smiled at her friend. Tracy was waxing so eloquent, and making great sense. She let Tracy wax on.

"Other people may be a little more spontaneous. They can connect with nature while out for a walk at noon. Or on their way to work. Some people can improvise inside the structure of their lives, like in jazz. It depends on the person and the circumstances. But to live in harmony means to make room for what is important to you. And when you do, balance comes with the rhythm and harmony. When you're balanced, the spiritual becomes a normal part of everyday life. I mean, you have to go to work. You have to work certain days, certain hours. So you can't just decide to take the day off because it's a beautiful day and you want to take in those flowering crab apple trees. But in the midst of your daily life, you still acknowledge earth's beauty. And make space for the spiritual."

They drank their skinny lattes, and Joan waited, hoping for more. Tracy swallowed and licked coffee from her lips. "A friend of mine always takes five minutes to be quiet and meditate when he gets back to his office after lunch. That isn't always at 1:00. But whenever it is, he takes five. He's acknowledging the spiritual. So it's about both harmony and balance. He validates what's important to him by giving it room—harmony. Then he works his values into the real schedule of his life—balance."

"I think I see, Tracy." Joan looked off into space, trying to catch up with what Tracy was saying. Suddenly Tracy scooted her chair back.

"I gotta go. My kids went to the Art Institute, and they don't have a huge attention span for the arts yet. See ya Monday."

After Tracy left, Joan got another latte. *That was a great conversation, but I'm exhausted. And hungry,* she suddenly realized as her stomach growled. Gosh, almost 1:00, no wonder. Joan returned to the counter for a sandwich. It would hold her until dinner, when she would meet Chip at Berghoffs, one of his favorite restaurants. It was his birthday, and she'd promised him the treat.

The next morning, a Sunday, Joan slept in until 7:30. She and Chip had enjoyed a great evening together and had talked late into the night. Throwing her terry robe around her, she went to the kitchen to fix coffee. While waiting for it to brew, she put some of her classical discs on with the two John Coltrane discs Tracy had loaned her, setting the CD player controls on random. She turned the music down low so she wouldn't rouse Chip, who would probably sleep till noon. His was the only room not connected with the stereo system in the house, since he had his own system, as well as his own very individual taste in music.

It was a peaceful morning. She heard only the soft gurgling of the coffeemaker and the lilting strains of Mozart. She filled her mug, sat down with her steaming brew, and began to leaf through the paper. As Joan read, the music swirled around her, first the structured symphonies and concertos of Bach and Handel, then Coltrane's free-floating harmonies and rhythms. Surrounded by the music, she spent the rest of the morning reading the Sunday paper and contemplating the previous day's conversation with Tracy.

The next day she met Tracy for lunch in the cafeteria. "When I put the very beautiful, but very structured classical music next to the freer, more soulful, individualized jazz, I could see how my life is like classical music—very structured, everything done within a pretty rigid framework. I wonder whether I could loosen up, be a little freer, like a jazz player. Live a little bit outside all the strict configurations with joy and playfulness." Joan's eyes smiled along with her mouth, something Tracy didn't often see.

Tracy grinned. "That's way cool, Joan."

Chapter 4
Twelve Notions

That year Chicagoans enjoyed a mild and pleasant summer. The very bearable humidity levels made for good lunchtime walking as well for after-work strolling to parking lots. Joan and Tracy met several more times at the book shop, either on Saturday mornings or for their Friday afternoon meeting, assured of some peace and privacy. The firm wasn't as frenzied in summer as during most of the year, so Joan felt comfortable working fewer hours, giving some time to her garden, mowing her own grass.

In late September law school began again for both Chip and Tracy. Chip was now out of the house, lodged at Northwestern University. And Joan's mentoring relationship with Tracy resumed. On Friday of the first week of school, when both were rushed after a long day and a hurried meeting, Joan said, "Well, I really have nothing more today. It's late. Do you have any concerns about school?"

"Well, yes, but I can't really talk about it now. I've got to get home."

"Can it wait till next week?"

"It's about an assignment for Wednesday."

"Oh, so you'll probably want to work on it this weekend. I have to come in tomorrow, unfortunately. Would you like to meet for coffee?"

"Sure. Ten o'clock?"

"You've got it."

Since becoming regulars, the women were greeted the next morning by several others who frequented the book cafe. Joan recalled the first time she and Tracy met there, how uncharacteristically self-conscious she had felt. Now she was very comfortable in Tracy's company. Both could maintain their professional comportment at work and get as much or more done than ever. But they occasionally shared inside jokes, or made remarks to each other incomprehensible to others in the office. Joan was aware of how important Tracy was becoming to her.

"Well, lady, what's up? You wanted to talk about school. Is the new semester getting off to a rough start?"

"Not particularly. It's just that I realized this week that I am at a crossroads. Everything about law school is hammering into you to be the best. Making the best grades, writing the best papers, succeed, succeed, succeed, and do it better than the next guy. You and I have talked about that. It's bothered me before, but this week I really got annoyed. The professor gave out a paper that named twelve characteristics common to lawyers. We can respond to it however we want, but we have to conclude it by analyzing the social and personal sacrifices and psychological adaptations each of us might have to make to become cutting-edge lawyers. We have to write about ourselves, and how we see our own lives in this process."

Tracy offered the paper to Joan, who dug in her purse for her reading glasses. "Twelve Notions about Lawyers According to Carl P. Koenig."

"Whew, this guy has some real interesting views about lawyers."

"Yeah, it's kind of critical the way he sees it."

"I can surely identify with some of these," Joan observed. "Like 'In interpersonal situations, lawyers are prone to disregard feelings and focus on facts.' Nothing new there. And this one, 'The adversarial nature of the law spills, disadvantageously, into non-law relationships. Lawyers are trained to be guarded and are reluctant to disclose fully.' That's one my therapist caught. I started working on that before the divorce. 'Because the client comes first, personal relationships necessarily come afterwards.' Lord knows, Charles and I were both guilty of that one. But this one here is kind of weird, 'Although lawyers are wedded to the truth, they are often not truthful interpersonally.' What the hell does that mean?"

"You tell me, lawyer lady," Tracy grinned.

"Some of these characteristics could be said of some *doctors* I know." Joan waggled her eyebrows significantly. "Like, 'Lawyers' capacity for sexual intimacy and mutual gratification is limited by the factors mentioned elsewhere. Often they are simply too busy or preoccupied.' I don't think lawyers have a corner on that one. But Tracy, this one really bothers me: 'Lawyers are selfish about success. They do not easily acknowledge staff and family support.' Am I like that?"

Tracy looked thoughtful. "No, Joan, I wouldn't say you are like that. At least not with me."

"Thank you. I hope not. I don't give credit to members of my family because, frankly, none of them has been very supportive. They don't appreciate how hard I've worked for the extras we have, or don't care, or balance it against the things I couldn't do because I was working." She found herself almost glaring at Tracy before lowering her eyes, self-conscious.

"Oh, well, enough of me. I can see why it bothered you. But a lawyer doesn't have to develop all of these characteristics, does she?"

"That's just the problem. The professor presented these like they were set in stone. Like if we become successful lawyers we can kiss satisfying personal relationships and marriage and family good-bye. Joan, I don't want that to happen to me. My family and friends are too important." Tracy smoothed her hair as if comforting it.

"Well, you certainly don't fit into this last one: 'The practice of law provides a refuge to those who have difficulty with ambivalent feelings and ambiguities in relationships. The law has precise, clearly defined rules, whereas non-law life has vague and inconsistent rules.' I mean, it's true that law has clear rules and non-law life often doesn't, but you don't seem to me to be the kind of person who is taking refuge from relationships in your pursuit of a career in law." Joan looked out the window for a moment .

"You know, Tracy, I'll bet a person's motives for going into law will have some affect on how these characteristics play out in her life. Why did you go into law?"

"That's a rather long story."

"That's okay. Tell me a story." Joan smiled.

"Well, it had a lot to do with my divorce and recovery. For a long time I couldn't get over my anger at Johnson, my ex-husband. I couldn't believe that he would leave me with our three children, just ditch us and leave me holding the bag. So I went to get some legal advice from a group on the South Side where I live. This group offers a number of services to the community, and I wanted help in tracking Johnson down and getting him to pay some child support. He didn't make much money, but every little bit was going to help. And I really wanted to nail him."

Joan grinned. She'd never before heard Tracy use any kind of strong language. "Sounds like you were really pissed off."

"You bet. What happened, though, is that the legal counselor began, very kindly, to explain to me what I already knew. That Johnson, who had grown up without models of men being in committed relationships, had no at-home father of his own.

"And yes, I could probably get a court order to make Johnson pay some child support, but given his rather fragile economic situation, it might make him homeless. In all likelihood, he would just not pay up, and that could land him in jail. The counselor asked me whether that was what I really wanted. At the time I thought I did, but I just shrugged. She asked me to think about it for a couple of weeks. She knew about my church involvement so she promised to pray for me. That astonished me."

"Wow." Joan shook her head, amazed. "If someone came to our firm, their lawyer would be out for blood. And have you ever heard of anyone in our firm praying for a client?"

"Yeah, I know. The Sunday after I talked with the lawyer, the pastor at Union Tab explained that the Gospel was very psychological and that Jesus offered psychological healing as well as physical and spiritual healing. His message moved me deeply. He invited people who wanted special prayers for inner healing to go forward to the alter. A lot of people went, including me."

Joan nodded encouragement.

"Then, after church, this marvelous, older woman, a pillar in the church, invited me to a healing service the next Wednesday evening. It's something that happens every week, hosted by the older, more mature, spiritual women in the church. It was a little awkward, because there were just two of us who were new. But these women were so kind, so warm. One motherly woman said, 'Let it go, child.' Another said, 'Reach for the gusto, Tracy.' And yet another, 'Healing is in his wings, baby. Trust him. Deliverance is here for you today.'"

Tracy's eyes glistened at the memory. "I just started bawling my eyes out. These beautiful black women stood up, came around me, put their hands on my head and shoulders and back. They prayed for my deliverance from anger and despair. They prayed for my forgiveness, and for my willingness to forgive my husband. They prayed for release of the emotional bonds that were tying me up inside. They prayed like they believed they were talking to a real person who could help. I learned later that they prayed from their own experiences of being delivered from pain and anger and despair."

Joan listened attentively, tears floating precariously at the edges of her own eyes—why? In admiration? In envy?

"After they prayed for a long time, maybe half an hour, they sang one of the most beautiful songs I have ever heard." Tracy sang the song softly. It was the first time Joan heard Tracy's beautiful, alto singing voice.

> We've come this far by faith
> Leaning on the Lord,
> Trusting in His Holy Word.
> Oh, Oh, Oh, we can't turn around,
> We've come this far by faith.

As Tracy sang, Joan ignored the curious glances of others in the coffee shop. Tracy didn't seem to notice.

"When they finished singing, they looked me over and said, 'Mmm, hmm. She's goin' to be okay now. Now child, daughter, we're so glad Jesus has healed you.'"

Joan swallowed hard. "That's powerful, Tracy."

"It was powerful. It changed my life."

Joan caught herself up short. Where were her powers of analysis? Her skepticism must have shown on her face for Tracy tapped her friend's wrist.

"Really, Joan. I know it sounds awfully religious, especially for an analytical, logical, thinking lawyer." Joan smiled, a bit embarrassed. Tracy continued. "That night I went home with a peace I hadn't experienced in a long time. I still had struggles. Still have struggles. But after two weeks I went back to the lawyer and told her I needed more time to think about my charges against Johnson."

"Man, Tracy, I'd want to get back at him. So I guess that prayer experience really did change you?"

"Yes it did. For a while I went back to the prayer circle every week for encouragement and prayer. Gradually my anger and bitterness against Johnson subsided. I tried to see him from the point of view of a God who loves him. I began to understand, not just know about, the limitations he had lived under all his life. After a couple of months, I told the lawyer at the Center to drop my case against Johnson."

"Amazing," was all Joan could manage.

"I was so impressed with the help that the lawyer at the South Side Center gave me that I thought I might like to be a lawyer someday and help people like she helped me."

"Kind of like deciding what you want to be when you grow up," Joan joked.

"Kind of. But remember, Joan, that in my upbringing people didn't often become lawyers or doctors. This woman at the South Side Center was the first lawyer I'd ever known, not to mention black or woman lawyer. She served as a model for a role I'd never imagined myself in. She encouraged me by saying I could do more for my community than filing and answering the phone, and that she'd help me with scholarship applications. So I decided to go for it."

"That took a lot of chutzpah, Tracy. Even with the scholarship, you still had to put food on the table and clothe yourself and your kids. You didn't have much money, I'm sure. What gave you the courage to make that decision?"

"My prayer group. That and the personal reading and meditating I was beginning to schedule regularly into my day. And the Center was amazing.

"They paid for my education at Martin Luther King Community College. I left my kids at the Center's daycare during the day, where they were fed two meals. In the evening I took my kids home and fixed dinner and got everyone to bed so we could do it all again the next day. The South Side Center made a huge contribution to our lives. I'll be forever grateful."

"I think I know the rest. You found out about the paralegal position in my office and applied."

"You got it. And see, Joan, it was only through the peace and confidence I'd received from my prayer group that I had the nerve to try this at all. And then, after I found the job working for you, I became convinced that law was something I have the ability to learn."

"I'd say so, definitely." Joan sipped her coffee feeling inexpressibly sad. "It must be hard for you to look at someone like me and wonder where a career in law will take you."

"Well, you don't exemplify all those negative characteristics in the article, Joan. Don't worry, you still model plenty of attributes someone like me can respect."

"That's good to hear. But I have to admit, I'm there in that list." Boisterous laughing erupted from the young crowd at the two tables next to them, making it impossible to continue the conversation for a moment. When it quieted down again, Joan continued.

"I'd say that you probably don't have to worry about becoming the lawyer your paper describes, Tracy. You already place a high value on relationships. You're not going into law to escape anything or to prove anything. I like that." Joan suddenly sat up straight and pointed at her friend. "And that's what you should write in your paper. Keep it straightforward and simple. You should tell your prof that you went into law to contribute to your community."

"You think that would be okay?"

"Absolutely. Tell him how it is for you. I don't know him, but I'll bet he's trying to complicate your focus by showing you all those lawyerly stereotypes. So tell him how his assumptions don't apply to you. Resist his static. Tell him truthfully what you think of his Twelve Notions. But be diplomatic." She grinned and glanced at her watch.

"Listen, Tracy, I have to get to the office. I'd be happy to look over a draft of your paper before you turn it into your professor."

"Thanks. I'll take you up on that."

As the two women went their separate ways, a flyer at the counter caught Joan's eye. A monk named Brother Theodore was to speak at Roosevelt University on "Identifying Your Inner Clutter." The ad defined inner clutter as anxiety, anger, guilt, obligations, obsessions, and addictions. Joan felt a prickle of recognition—hadn't she just been telling Tracy to focus and simplify? She made a mental note to point out the lecture to Tracy. Maybe they could go together. Underneath the ad was a short article that Joan resolved to read later as she folded the flyer and stuffed it into her purse.

Joan didn't leave the office until 5:00, a little resentful at having spent so much time inside on a gorgeous day, and now a thunderstorm was brewing. It was raining by the time she arrived home. And of course the days were shorter now, and it was already dark. She fixed herself a salad and cut a couple of slices of the hearty bread that she had made yesterday in her bread maker. Miffed at being cheated out of a fine fall day, she consoled herself with a White Russian, put on her John Coltrane CD (she had long since returned Tracy's to her and purchased her own), kicked off her shoes, and curled up in her favorite chair. She pulled the article out of her purse and started to read.

> If you are approaching fifty, or have reached or passed it, you are probably wondering how you got to this place in your life. Where did the last twenty or thirty years go? You recall vividly the sixties and seventies, the years when you were determined to save the world.

Today, in midlife, your attention has turned more inward. You are beginning to evaluate the kind of life you are leading. Perhaps you are beginning to assess whether the values and commitments you have now will sustain you into the future. If you probe the choices you have made so far, you may realize that the external accomplishments that once meant so much to you cannot substitute for the inner quality of life you need now. You are interested in developing an integrated spirituality that deals with the realities of your life and the world you live in, a world very different from the world of your young adulthood.

You are beginning to recognize the clutter stifling your spirit—appointments, phone calls, expectations of others, expectations of yourself, disappointments, setbacks, guilt, sorrow. You are seeking ways to attain spiritual balance and internal, as well as external, freedom.

Thursday evening Brother Theodore, from a Benedictine monastery in the desert of Southern California, will speak about how to begin freeing ourselves from internal clutter. Once a practicing psychotherapist, he now weaves Jungian principles with spiritual disciplines.

Brother Theodore contends that anyone may cultivate spirituality. It is possible for people on the road, in the marketplace, working in every context. Spirituality is for the daily grind, for the

> ups and downs, for the difficulties, problems, burdens, and frustrations of life. And he believes it begins by recognizing internal clutter and noise—whatever has deadened us to what is inside us, where God wants to live.
>
> Hear his lecture at Roosevelt University at 7:30 on Thursday.

She began to think about her conversation with Tracy. *I didn't have to go to work or get into a career. I guess I needed to feel like somebody important. We're all strivers, those of us who have succeeded in the top-end firms. I don't think I realized that it would take so much from me.*

She reread "Twelve Notions About Lawyers," again resenting the man's presumptions, but finally admitting that he was spot on. He might have known her. She looked again at the article. That too was very perceptive. She probably had a ton of clutter inside. She could practically hear it rattling around.

Chapter 5
An Old Monk

The more she thought about the lecture, the more intrigued Joan became. On Monday, during a quick lunch with Tracy, Joan had to work to keep her voice casual.

"Oh, by the way. I found an interesting article Saturday at the bookstore." Joan pulled it out of her purse. "You might be interested in reading it. It's really a push for a lecture Thursday night at Roosevelt University about internal clutter. Have you ever heard of internal clutter?"

"Sure."

"Wanna go together?" Joan wondered what she would do if her new friend said no.

"Mmm, this is interesting." Tracy said after glancing at the ad.

"How about grabbing a bite to eat first?"

"Great. I'll put it on the schedule." Joan almost laughed with relief. She and Tracy disposed of their garbage and recyclables and caught the elevator together.

Thursday was hectic for both women. Tracy was in court all morning, and Joan met a client in Elmhurst. In the afternoon, they worked together on a case that would be presented at court on the following Monday. Time grew short. *If I hadn't already invited Tracy to the lecture, I might skip tonight,* thought Joan. *I could really use the time to catch up.* But finally they both reached a place in their work where they could reasonably break. They filed away papers, cleaned up their desks, and scooted themselves out the door at 6:15. They ran down the six flights of stairs rather than waiting for a crowded elevator.

It was still rush hour in the city, and it took a good half-hour for the hurrying women to get to Roosevelt University, and another fifteen minutes to find the auditorium. It was pretty full, but there were still seats together about midway down the center aisle. As a distinguished-looking man at the podium quieted the audience, Joan led the way to two seats. Settling in, Joan closed her eyes, took a deep breath, and tried to quiet herself. *I sure hope this lecture helps—something.* The old monk was being introduced. There was applause.

When she opened her eyes, Joan saw a tall, white-haired man rise from his chair and slowly make his way to the podium. He moved with great dignity, looking out kindly on the audience. When he reached the lectern, he stood for a moment gazing out at the crowd as if in appraisal. Even from where she was, Joan could see that Brother Theodore's eyes sparkled blue under shaggy white eyebrows. Though his skin was wrinkled and he was slightly stooped, he struck Joan as being quite alert, energetic, full of life.

"Good evening," he began in a deep, rich, kind voice.

"As we have embarked upon the twenty-first century, our lives as never before are full of clutter and noise. Clutter and noise do not happen overnight As we grow older, we accumulate things. We purchase new tools and clothes and books, and then we discover that we need a larger space to accommodate our goods. What began as a pile on the desk soon becomes a full file cabinet, and then a full closet, and then a full room. Before long we are buried under the weight of accumulated things. You know, all those kitchen gadgets, the three or four different kinds of vacuum cleaners."

People in the audience chuckled.

"We bow under the load of our possessions like a figure out of Dante's *Inferno*. Our bodies sag as our possessions increase, and we lose the light step and the carefree skip of an earlier age. But even more significant than the physical clutter of our lives is our spiritual clutter. Our physical clutter is only a sign of the spiritual load we bear. We carry massive loads of guilt with us—guilt for not spending enough time with the children, guilt for not caring adequately for aging parents, guilt for faithlessness toward a spouse. The weight of the burden increases with a need for forgiveness, dreams deferred and abandoned, injuries inflicted and suffered, abuse experienced, bad choices, and sorrow piled upon sorrow. In frustration, we cry with the Psalmist of the Old Testament, "Save me, O God, for the waters have come up to my neck." (Psalm 69:1, *NKJV*)

Here Theodore paused. He looked affectionately out at the hushed crowd for a moment. Joan, eyes wide, shoulders forward, held her breath.

"Let me tell you my story," Theodore resumed in an Irish brogue softened through the years, but still distinct, "and about the clutter that I accumulated, some of it thrust upon me, much of it dragged willfully through my life, until it broke me. Until I surrendered to healing from the internal noise and clutter and devastation that I had accumulated over the years, since childhood.

"I was born in 1928, between the two world wars. My early childhood was bleak. When I was three years old, my father died and left my mother very poor. In working hard to provide for me, she broke her own health and died when I was only seven years old.

"A Catholic orphanage took me in. The people charged with my care were very kind and very pious. They brought me up in the church and gave me opportunities to be an altar boy and to sing in the boys' choir. There I learned basic Christian doctrine as well as the spiritual disciplines of prayer, meditation, and reflection. I began to open up and trust again. I went on to study history at the University of Dublin. It was then that I became fascinated with the history of Europe during the Middle Ages, which of course includes the history of the church. One of my professors was so pleased with my work that he persuaded a wealthy friend of his to put me through graduate school in Oxford. I earned a Ph.D. in medieval studies.

"During this time in Oxford I met, at the home of one of my professors, a lovely young Irish woman named Granné."

He trilled the *r* as he said the name. "It's a name you don't have on this side of the pond, but it's lovely, don't you think?"

The audience murmured agreement.

"I was so taken with her that I finally made time for some social life. Granné and I fell in love and married the week after I received my doctorate. God blessed us with a beautiful little girl we named Maria. Rea for short. She had strawberry blonde curls and big green eyes and dimples in her plump little cheeks. And she loved her papa."

Theodore's voice caught for just a moment, and he paused briefly before continuing. "I felt that I had more joy than I could contain. My life was full. Clutter for me then was a matter of easy choices. You know, clutter can be a bunch of good things, too. The kinds of clutter I faced then were choices about whether to go to the pub tonight or stay home and spend the evening with my wife, or what to select as a surprise gift for my daughter.

"When Rea was only three years old, she and Granné were killed in an automobile accident."

Joan shivered. She glanced over at Tracy who glanced back in amazement, her eyes bright.

Theodore continued.

"Once again I felt the crushing sense of abandonment. Believing that God had utterly forsaken me, I not only left the Catholic church; I rejected all religion. I convinced myself that God was not interested in the affairs of mortals. That he had breathed life into creation, then left the world to tip out of control on its own. I closed my heart to God and to trusting—God or anyone else.

"I then began to collect the clutter that would fill my mind and my spirit. I left Dublin to accept a position as medievalist at the Sorbonne in France. For fifteen years I tried to deaden my pain by chasing pleasure then salving my conscience in various ways. I taught all day, caroused many nights. Paris is a good place for that. But my hurt would not die. The pain still pulsated in a dark corner of my soul. I became restless and tired of my life. The offer of a position at Harvard University gave me an opportunity to make another change. I hoped this change would help still the inner clamor and noise.

"This was in 1968. At Harvard, I became friends with some psychologists and began dabbling in psychological theory, first as a hobby, then as a way to uncover and destroy the pain inside."

Joan straightened up, her back starting to ache from her stiff position. She saw Tracy uncross her legs and change positions too, but Tracy looked less intense than Joan felt.

"While I continued to teach medieval studies with a lightened class load, I began to study psychology formally, and in the process of earning my Ph.D. in psychoanalysis was introduced to Carl Jung. At first he was only one of many in the field who intrigued me.

"Though I began a successful psychotherapy practice, I became more and more aware of a great inner emptiness. Or what I thought was emptiness. It was really more of a longing, and I discovered, to my surprise, that I wasn't empty inside at all. Inside I was full of clutter. Psychological debris. Anger. Guilt. Depression. Those feelings of abandonment. Betrayal.

"I turned more and more to the writings of Carl Jung, who wrote so eloquently: "We are shaken by secret shudders and dark forebodings; but we know no way out, and very few persons indeed draw the conclusion that this time the issue is the long-since-forgotten soul of man." The forgotten soul. Indeed, I knew about soul from my Catholic upbringing. Indeed I had forgotten. From Jung I recaptured the concept of an inner life or soul. Out of the depths of my anguish, out of the internal clutter and noise of my despair and the deeper emptiness they created, I began to turn back to God. I gradually realized that

God hadn't left me after all. He was always there. Right where I had left Him."

Brother Theodore's voice was an intense whisper as he leaned toward the microphone. He continued in a normal voice.

"I took an extended spiritual retreat at the Benedictine monastery where I now reside. There, through the compassionate and patient direction of an old monk named Brother Christopher, I learned to acknowledge God in all of life.

"I learned again to pray, and during many prayers of silence God began to show me the pain that walled me off from myself, from my feelings, from life, from Himself."

Joan sat riveted, totally unaware of anything or anyone except the old monk. She felt he was talking directly to her as he continued.

"The rest of my story is fairly straightforward. I reconnected with the Roman Catholic Church from which I was discovering new life, and I became a Benedictine monk. Today I am committed to using the gifts of both psychology and spirituality to help men and women like yourselves find their inner core, meet God, and become whole people as God intended."

The monk paused to take a sip of water from the glass tumbler on the corner of his lectern. When he put it down, he took a moment to once again scan the audience.

"Noise and clutter, like ravenous twins, feed upon each other. The noise tells you how inadequate your life is. So you purchase and accumulate in order to become adequate and happy. But the accumulation only produces clutter, which, in turn, creates a sense of unease and unhappiness. You ignore the message by listening to the noise again, which assures you that if you just get one more thing your life will be full. Each time the cycle repeats, you are left with emptiness, aimlessness, and a vague sense that all is not well

"The results of the clutter and noise are the *loss of integrity*. The very things that culture touts as sources of integrity result in loss of integrity. Things complicate people's lives, tear them, fracture them, rather than helping them simplify, mend, and make them whole.

"But let me clarify. Complexity itself is not necessarily clutter. For example, in business, there are multiple tasks—phones ringing, messages, reports, research, to do lists, assignments, administrative duties, and so forth. These are all necessary and productive, but they do complicate life. We always live in tension between the essential and nonessential stuff of life. It's when complexity becomes overwhelming, unmanageable, unsafe, or unhealthy that it truly becomes clutter, which annoys, confuses, creates havoc, dissonance, distraction, and turmoil.

"People think they can orchestrate 'quality time' with their families by scheduling them into their busy lives, which are ordered by the clock and the ever-present daily planner. Anxiety and hurriedness are the norm and make havoc of inner peace and serenity, which become litter along the landscape of our lives."

Tracy nudged Joan and smiled. Joan winked in response.

"A psychotherapist friend of mind recently invited me to one of his therapy groups to discuss this issue of internal clutter. Everyone seemed to know immediately what clutter was all about. Their lives were littered with pain, confusion, busyness, and bitterness. One woman can't throw anything away because she fears letting go of past love. Her spirit jangles from a life without unconditional love.

"Another person can never commit to personal relationships for fear of repeating the deep disappointments of her childhood. Her past is littered with broken trust. Still another is embarrassed by his nationality, and now lives in relative isolation because he cannot let anyone know who he truly is and where he's come from. There's the clutter of shame.

"A young woman quietly risked telling the strangers around her who she is and what she has suffered. She hopes for acceptance and some kind of meaning from the years of sexual, emotional, and physical abuse.

"One thing is certain about psychological clutter—there is no rest within it.

"Consider this: a good friend of mine has a lovely old oak table. For years he carefully polished, guarded, and enjoyed the table as a fine antique. Now it receives all the mail, messages, unfinished business, half-read books, and bills.

"In the midst of all this clutter, a lovely schefflera plant thrives. It becomes difficult to even find it on the table, much less enjoy the beauty of the plant. But it keeps growing, indifferent to the chaos around it. Something apart from the messy table allows it to grow.

"That plant is like our spirits. Even when we ourselves are working hard to eliminate inner clutter, the clutter outside, all around us, clamors for our attention, threatens to invade our inner lives. But like that plant, our spirits can grow and flourish when we tend to what is truly important in our lives.

"Permit me one more analogy.

"You know, I love music. I learned classical music in my traditional education in Britain. I didn't think much of jazz and blues and other forms of American music until I moved here some years ago."

Joan had begun to feel sleepy, and she had heard Tracy try to stifle a yawn. But suddenly both women took notice, glancing quickly at each other, then looking straight ahead. Brother Theodore continued.

"But when I moved to America I became friends with an African-American musician. Oh, he knew the classical rules. He knew the timing and the notes and the measures. He knew all about the structure of classical music. He had been given a top-notch education in classical music. But he was a jazz musician.

"He explained to me that he had gravitated to jazz because, though he loves classical music, his spirit needs a more expressive medium. You see, in classical music, you're supposed to play the music the way the composer intended it as closely as you can.

"In jazz, by contrast, the musician uses the written music as a starting point. He is free to take that written music wherever his insides lead him that day. And how he plays it today is different from the way he will play it tomorrow. The way he plays the music on any given day expresses what is inside him at that moment.

"Just now, I would like to improvise on a passage from the Bible, Psalm One. I'd like to do this in the form of a meditation. Please just sit back and listen with all your being. And if you fall asleep, that's okay. You probably need it."

Joan, now on her second wind, sat up straight, but closed

her eyes and strained her ears for all the improvisational nuances, the way she'd learned to hear John Coltrane.

"Blessed is the person who ignores the siren call to accumulate wealth or possessions, or to keep more than is really necessary, or tolerate those who judge people by their possessions. That person instead delights in the things which God ordained to nurture the soul of human beings. On these he meditates day and night.

"That person shall be like the plant amid the clutter on the table. The plant is watered daily and fed by the positive nourishment of those things that are truly important—Scripture, meditation, quietness, prayer, attention to the soul. This plant brings forth its fruit in its season. Its leaf will not whither. This plant will prosper.

"Say the oak table is your life. Is its clutter stifling you? Or are you the plant that lives in the midst of it, but is not attached to it, not dependent on it for life? Are you the plant whose inner life is being healed every day from the clutter inside because it finds nourishment in those things that it was meant to feed on? And thus nourished, can you thrive amid the clutter and noise and chaos and cacophony of the outer world?"

As he spoke, Joan knew again that he was talking right to her.

After the lecture Tracy kissed her friend quickly on the cheek and left immediately. It was quite late since Brother Theodore had taken questions after his talk. But Joan stood in a long line just to shake the old man's hand and thank him. As she approached, she found herself asking for a personal appointment.

"I can't do it tonight," the old man responded, seeming to

recognize something in Joan's urgency. "I wouldn't be giving you the attention you deserve. But I could meet you tomorrow morning for coffee at the café downstairs. Say 8:00?"

Without thinking about the mound of paper on her desk, Joan agreed.

Later at home, she left Tracy a voice message at the office letting her know she would be late for work the next day.

Chapter 6
Invitation

Joan turned her light out and put her head onto the pillow. It was almost one o'clock. Though she had gotten home two hours earlier, she had not even tried to go to sleep—she was too wound up. She kept remembering what the old monk had said about jazz. How eerily similar it was to that conversation with Tracy last summer! When she tried to think about something else, she reflected on Theodore's story—all the losses, all the tragedy—yet how he seemed so together.

She had tried to do a little work when she got home to help her calm down a bit. She had read and reread the first paragraph of the brief she was preparing and finally had given up. Then she had turned on CNN to see whether there was any late-breaking news to distract her. No. She'd already heard everything they had to say.

Even after she turned out her light, sleep eluded her. She realized she was getting nervous about the conversation the next morning with this monk. What had she gotten herself into? She had nothing to say to him. Nothing at all to offer. She sure wasn't going to tell him her life story, like he had done in front of that crowd. *That took a lot of guts. What right did he have to unburden himself on all of them?* She couldn't get that story out of her mind. *Who did he think he was that he thought everyone would be interested? And if I'm not interested, how come I'm still thinking about him!*

Joan got up to get some antacid tablets for the heartburn beginning in her stomach. How she wished she hadn't made that stupid appointment! Well, she had, and now she needed to go to sleep so she wouldn't be totally fried tomorrow—today. What she really needed now was a cigarette, and not a one in the house. She'd already sneaked all of the ones she'd hidden for emergencies. *And I'm NOT going to go out now to get a pack.*

Finally her conscious mind fell into a restless doze, but even in sleep her nervous apprehension dogged her. Once she woke up in a cold sweat, unable to recall the dream she knew she had just had. Another time she woke up crying. She tossed and turned for a couple more hours, finally giving it up at 4:00. Then she began to dread in earnest the meeting ahead of her.

Since she couldn't sleep, she may as well be awake. She fixed a pot of coffee. Once again she opened her briefcase—and closed it again. Instead, she would watch a video. Something light. But the noise in her head overcame the voices of *Out of Africa*. The music only formed a backdrop for her thoughts.

What was I thinking? Besides all the work I have to do today, what am I going to say to him? We aren't even on the same wavelength, not really. What he said got to me, but that's probably all he knows to talk about. Joan checked herself, remembering his impressive résumé and life story. *What did he say he'd studied? Theology? Well, I sure don't know anything about that. Psychology? Bzzt, wrong. Not my field. History? Hmm. Maybe we could talk about history.* She smirked to herself. *Right. I'll bet that's NOT what he expects to talk about. Does he have an agenda? I sure don't.*

What might his agenda be? Does he want me to spill my guts? He's outta luck. I'm sure not ready for confession! Why am I drawn to him? I've never done anything like this before. What was I thinking? I'm not going to pour out my soul to someone I hardly know. I wish I could cancel, but I can't call him now. Besides all the work I have to do. I guess I'll just have to follow through.

Finally, it was time to shower and dress. The shower cleared her head a bit. She blew her hair dry and put on a crisp white cotton blouse and her smartly tailored charcoal suit. Power dressing always made her feel a little more in control. Maybe it would help her keep the monk at a psychological distance.

Brother Theodore was waiting for her at the street level coffee shop at Roosevelt University. He stood when he saw her, smiled, remained standing as she approached.

"Good morning, Joan. How are you?"

"Fine, thank you. Uh, is it Brother Theodore?"

"Yes. Brother is fine. I've already gotten my tea and crumpets. Feel free to get something for yourself before we get started."

"Thanks, I will."

Joan selected a sugar-coated cinnamon roll and a bottle of orange juice. She'd already had plenty of coffee this morning. She returned to their table where Brother Theodore was holding her chair. *Such a gentleman.* She smiled and let him seat her.

"It's good to see you, Joan."

"Thank you."

"Joan, what do you do?"

"I'm a lawyer."

"Have you been a lawyer long?"

"Well, I passed the bar when I was twenty-four, almost twenty-five. I clerked for a while for Federal Judge Payne. Then

I connected with my current firm and have been there ever since. Since I'm forty-eight now, I guess that makes me a lawyer for twenty-three years. That's a long time; I don't know where the years have gone," she said a bit ruefully and smiled at the old man.

"You started quite young."

"I did both high school and college in three years. I married the summer between college graduation and starting law school. Then our first child was born before our second anniversary. The next one came just after law school, then the third one a year and a half after that."

"Sounds like you plunged right into your early adulthood."

"Yeah. It was probably dumb planning. Or no planning." She smiled, a little embarrassed. She felt like a schoolgirl next to him. At the same time, she felt great respect for the impressive old man.

"What does your husband do?" asked Brother Theodore.

"My ex-husband is a pediatric heart specialist."

"I'm sorry. I didn't mean to pry." He spoke softly with a kind smile on his mouth and in his eyes. "How long have you been divorced?"

"It's been two and a half years. Not very long. But long enough to get used to it, I guess."

Brother Theodore momentarily looked down at the bagel he was buttering, then looked up again. "That must have been a difficult transition."

Joan felt herself softening. This man she didn't know really did seem to care.

"It was. It was pretty much of a surprise on my part. It left me in shock. When that wore off I guess I was pretty angry for a long time."

"Yes, you must have gone through all those stages of grief we talk about."

"Yeah, well . . . Brother Theodore, I really don't want to talk about that if you don't mind."

"Certainly. What would you like to talk about? Would you mind telling me why you came to the lecture last night? What drew you?"

"Well, I saw an ad and article in a small local paper. I thought it would be interesting."

"Mm-hmm." Brother Theodore waited for her to go on. And waited. Finally, "That was all? Just that you saw the article?"

"Well, a friend and I had talked about having rhythm, harmony, and balance in life. What the flyer said about inner clutter seemed to relate. Like the opposite of rhythm, harmony, balance. I'd never thought of clutter as internal. I thought my friend would be interested."

"I see. And did you like the talk?"

"Um, yes. It was interesting."

"Anything in particular stand out to you?"

"Well," Joan hesitated. This guy was breaking down some of her defenses. She didn't know if that was good or bad, but she needed desperately to keep control of this conversation. "The whole concept of clutter being something internal, something psychological. I just think that's a novel concept. According to your definitions, I'm just full of clutter." Joan laughed a little shrill laugh.

Brother Theodore smiled again. "We all are. That's why that lecture always draws a crowd." A pause.

"Do you and your friend talk about life issues often?"

"Not until last May." Joan held her cup aloft almost in front of her face, looking at it. *If this guy is determined to see inside me he's going to have to work for it.*

Brother Theodore carefully laid his butter knife on his plate, so gently that it made no noise. "What happened in May? Do you want to talk about it?"

Joan hesitated. She had not meant to get into this. But here she was. And why else did she want to talk to him anyway? She finally began, "Well, last May when my ex got married again, I had a hard time with it. I thought it would help to go up to the cabin we used to own—I got that piece of our marriage—and I took a couple of colleagues with me. Thought it would take my mind off the pain. But it didn't. I found I could take myself out of the noisy, cluttered city, but I couldn't escape the noise and clutter inside me. Hey, that was pretty good, wasn't it?"

"You're getting it," Brother Theodore nodded with a smile.

"Anyway, something kind of shook inside me. I got all emotional and angry the first night there when I thought my two friends were asleep. I guess I cursed and cried and gushed a bit by myself. They must have heard most of it; it was kind of embarrassing. But it seemed like something started to open up inside me that night. There was this hole inside. Tracy and I ended up talking about some things, and we've kind of continued that conversation since."

"And Tracy is the friend you brought to the lecture last night?"

"Yes."

"And she works with you? How does she relate to you at work?"

"She's my paralegal. And she is great at her job. Very meticulous. Very bright. Wants to be a lawyer herself, to help people from the South Side where she came from."

"Interesting. Perhaps she has found a mission, or a calling."

"That's what I told her."

"Oh, you did? That's interesting. So do you see law as mission for you?"

"Humph. I don't think so."

"What is your profession to you?"

"What do you mean?"

"If you don't see it as a mission, do you see it as a way to perform, to prove yourself? To become wealthy?"

"Oh. I don't know. I guess it just seemed a logical thing to do. I love history. Politics. Have an interest in business. It just seemed like a good way to use my abilities and my education. And yes, there was the attraction of a good lifestyle as a reward for hard work and success."

"Has it been satisfying for you?" Brother Theodore's voice was still soft, but there was no mistaking the heat of his scrutiny.

Boy is he persistent. "In many ways yes. I do it well. That's satisfying. I do make a decent living, have a nice house. And in the process, help a few people. And make a few enemies here and there, but that goes with the territory." She ended the sentence with a mutter.

"Oh? And what territory is that?"

Joan looked at him. Had he really been listening? She replied sternly, "The territory of a successful attorney."

"And you help people in your work."

"Hopefully, yes. Many times I do."

"But your rewards are primarily material?" he asked.

"Well, I guess primarily. Material success. But it's rewarding to be able to put your whole self into your work."

"And you are able to do that?"

"Well, usually, yes."

"So everything you are and offer is utilized in your practice of law."

"I think I already said yes." Joan was getting irritated. All these questions. *Of course I like my job, am rewarded by my job. Would I do it otherwise?*

"Do you feel you have had to give up anything, any part of yourself that you value, in order to be successful in your job?"

"Umm." Joan looked away from him to her plate, the cinnamon roll barely touched. "I don't know. Like what?"

"Well, I'd like you to tell me. Are you satisfied with life as it has developed for you? Is everything you value in harmony? Are you as satisfied with, just for example, your family life as you are with your professional life?"

Boy, he just went for the jugular. "Well, I guess I told you about my marriage. No, of course that wasn't satisfying. That was very disappointing. So I've recovered. And I move on."

"And your children—they must be a comfort to you."

Where is he going with this? "Um, well, I could have done a better job with them. See, I can't do too many things at one time like some people seem able to do. So I committed myself to my profession, and I guess I hoped for the best. They could have turned out worse. I mean, they aren't on drugs—that I know of. They are all making sound decisions in college; they seem to know who they are. Not that I can accept all of the credit for that. But they're fine."

"Do you wish you could have done more than one thing at a time?"

"I guess I haven't thought of it much. I don't see where you are going with this."

"I guess I'm trying to get back to the hole you said you felt opening up inside you. I didn't do a very good job. So let me just say, can we talk about that for a minute?"

"I guess. I'm not sure what I can tell you about that."

"I don't expect you to be able to explain it necessarily."

"You seemed to do so well describing your experience. I don't think I can articulate mine that clearly."

"Don't worry about that. Believe me, when I first started talking to someone about my clutter, I didn't sound like I did last night."

Another silence before Brother Theodore continued, "So the hole."

"Yes. So the hole. Well, I don't even know how to talk about it. Maybe you've put your finger on it. Maybe it is something about the money and prestige and success being not quite enough. Maybe I expected it to be enough. Maybe it really isn't after all. But I really want it to be."

"Why? Why do you want it to be enough?"

"To validate all the hard work and . . ."

"And?"

"Well, I hate to use the word sacrifice, it sounds so dramatic somehow. I don't see my decisions as being sacrifices. Gosh, I'm usually more articulate than this in front of people. You've got me thinking out loud, Brother Theodore."

"Oh, Heaven forbid." They both chuckled. Then another silence.

"This is really difficult for some reason." Joan took a deep breath.

Brother Theodore came to her rescue. "Joan, have you ever spent much time thinking about the meaning of life?"

"Brother Theodore, I really am not interested in religion, if that's what you're talking about."

Brother Theodore looked at her and grinned, a twinkle in his eye. "Now, Joan, I didn't ask you if you were religious, or interested in religion. I asked whether you've ever thought about the meaning of life. Why are we here?" He looked at Joan and the grin got bigger. "I'll bet you think I'm setting you up."

"How did you guess?" replied Joan with an edge on her voice.

"Well, I can see why you would think that. I only wanted to hear you talk more about what's getting at you, that you were intrigued by a lecture on inner clutter, that you would confess to feeling some kind of hole inside. I was just trying to help you talk a little more about that."

"I guess I'm not used to talking this way. It's a bit uncomfortable."

"Sure. I understand. Forgive me if I've forced the issue."

"That's okay."

"Well, maybe I should start again. You brought it up so let me ask outright. Have you ever been religious?"

"It's funny you should ask. Like I told Tracy, I went to church when I was young, but not since I was ten years old. When we moved to the Gold Coast we kind of quit. I spent Sundays sometimes in the park near our home being what I guess was as close to religious as I could be without church."

"How do you mean?"

"Well, I enjoyed spending time out in nature. At the park I would find a picnic table and read poetry, journal, write some poetry. Sometimes for literature classes, but often for my own entertainment."

"Do you write any more?"

"Nah. Law school and my law career kind of wiped out any propensity I had for the poetic."

"Do you ever miss it?"

"Hmm. I really haven't thought about it for quite a while. But up at the cabin I realized that I hadn't even noticed nature for a long time. When Tracy and I took a walk after my angry evening on the porch, I realized it had been a long time since I had even felt the wind blow through my hair. A long time since I had noticed and enjoyed the reawakening of spring. It was a little like something was waking up inside me."

"Really? Talk a little more about that."

"There's not much more to tell. It's like something was waking up. Something internal. It's yawning. And it's hungry, I guess."

"Good. You're getting there."

"Getting where?"

"You're explaining something that is hard to explain. You say something is waking up inside. But does something have to go to sleep before it wakes up?"

"Well, yeah, if you put it that way. I suppose some part of me could have gone into hibernation." She laughed uncomfortably.

Brother Theodore looked at her over his teacup as he drank. Then he said, "Hibernation might be a good way to put it. A bear that hibernates, wakes up at the end of winter crabby, hungry, insistent on finding something to fill his stomach after a long fast."

"Well, hibernation may be a good description, but I don't sense that kind of hunger, at least not yet."

Brother Theodore popped the last bit of his bagel into his mouth and chewed, eyes on the table. After swallowing he looked to the other side of the coffee shop for a moment. Then he looked back at Joan.

"There's another way to look at it, Joan. And let's give that thing inside a name, just for reference. Let's call it your soul."

"Yes, Jung's forgotten soul."

"Very good. You really were listening last night. So your soul. To me, the wakening of the soul can be less like the sudden awakening of a hungry bear and more like a seed starting to germinate after being dormant for a long time. Say it's been resting beneath a sidewalk, or in a tiny crevasse between mortar and a brick in a building. But when spring rains come, hairlike tentacles creep persistently forth from the seed, filling up that little crevasse and sneaking unobserved around the corners of the bricks and into tiny spaces in the mortar. Eventually it attaches to the wall of the building. If left undisturbed, in a year or two it can wreak havoc on the building, creating cracks in the walls and compromising the structure. It's a silent, slow process, but there is great force in it.

"That's the kind of force that a waking soul can have on an individual. Quiet, invisible at first. Perhaps dormant for years. But something wakens it. Often a crisis like divorce or the approach of middle age. The soul begins to stir. If it is ignored, it will make itself known anyway."

Joan sat still, staring at Brother Theodore. Finally, "That's quite poetic. Descriptive."

Brother Theodore looked at her again over his teacup, his eyes benign. "Perhaps, Joan, there are walls that the seed of your soul is trying to break through. I don't know. You have to discover that. And be willing to allow it to grow. That seed can be deterred from its growth, or it can be stopped, at least for a time. You have to decide whether you are willing to allow that seed to grow and to help it along by nourishing it."

"It sounds a bit scary." Now Joan understood why she had feared this conversation. Could she face the abyss of change?

"Yes. Growth often is scary. But usually it brings us to a better place in our lives if we cooperate with it."

"Hmmm."

"Listen, Joan, I have to go. I see my ride to the airport over there." He leaned over his briefcase then straightened up again. "Here is my card. You know, I don't accept every request for a private conversation that I get. I neither have the time nor the inclination to do so. I try to discern whether someone is really searching for something more in their life. I don't mean to put words in your mouth, but I sense that you may be ready to look at some issues in your life. That you may, as you said, be waking up inside. Often a waking soul needs some kind of guidance. I do what is called spiritual direction. I help waking, troubled souls in their search for meaning. I would like to invite you to think about spending a week at my monastery. We could spend extended times of conversation together, I could recommend some reading, and so on. You could come as my guest, take a private room at the monastery, eat with the monks and other pilgrims.

"You could join us for daily prayers if you wish, though it's not a requirement. You'd have access to our excellent library. I could meet with you twice a day to talk about what you are thinking and feeling. I would give you little assignments, pieces of spiritual literature to read and respond to. You'd keep a journal of your experience, which you'd be welcome to share with me or not, as you wish. We're just forty miles outside San Diego, and you could rent a car at the airport. Your food and shelter would be taken care of, no charge. Think about it and write to me when you are ready to talk about specifics.

"I have no private telephone for you to call, and no e-mail address. If you want to get hold of me, you have to do it the old-fashioned way—you have to write. And send it U.S. Postal Service. But as you think about our conversation, if you think you would like to spend a concentrated amount of time investigating what is going on inside and discovering how to nourish it, write me a note. Write me anyway, whenever you feel like it, if you have something you'd like to run by me. But please consider taking a week away, maybe in the winter when Chicago isn't so nice and the desert is truly a retreat."

Joan took her own card from her wallet and gave it to him.

"Thank you. Now I really must run." He stood and Joan followed suit, taking his proffered hand and shaking it as they maintained extended eye contact. Then he picked up his briefcase and was gone.

Joan sat back down and stayed there for a few moments without moving. It seemed that the world stood still. She fingered Brother Theodore's card, then put it in her wallet. She suddenly became aware of the noise in the coffee shop, which had increased in volume since they had first met. Chattering and laughing students lined up to order their coffee and goodies, and sat in groups at tables around her. Joan looked at her watch. *Good grief. 9:45. I gotta get moving.*

She grabbed her briefcase and left their dishes on the table. Walking quickly she left the coffee shop and headed to the bus stop. It was a cool, crisp day, and Joan changed her mind about the bus. Chicago had few enough of these days in a year. She would walk to the office today; that would probably get her there as quickly as the bus. As she walked, she caught sight of the broken, bent body of a homeless man hovering in the doorway of a building. He looked dirty, matted, scruffy. Joan felt a tug at her heart, pausing momentarily to acknowledge him, before hurrying on her way. Then it dawned on her how out of character it was for her to notice that man. She had seen another human being, one less successful, less prosperous than she. And she had felt something for him. She saw homeless people all the time, and walked on by. Why was this time different?

Chapter 7
A Wakening

It was the third Tuesday in October, Joan's favorite month. After a rather grueling day, Joan was on her way home looking forward to unwinding. She didn't often, but tonight she left her work at the office. She just needed to relax. It had been weeks since their encounter, but she'd been thinking about Brother Theodore. She really should write him a letter. At first she'd dismissed the whole idea of going to a monastery as frivolous, but as the firm resumed its hectic fall pace, she'd been mulling the possibility over again and again.

When she arrived home, Joan made herself a White Russian, put John Coltrane's *Ballads* on again, drew water for a bath, poured in English lavender aromatherapy crystals, and lit three English lavender-scented candles sitting on the window ledge beside the tub. The strains of the gentle, sensuous, fluid music, the light brush and beat of the percussion began soothing her. She tried to concentrate on each sense—seeing the flickering candles; inhaling the English lavender of her bath; tasting the smooth, delicate drink; sensing the warm, aromatic water touching and licking her in the most intimate ways; and the languid light feeling the drink gave her. She savored the comfort, feeling a peacefulness and a serenity that she had not felt in many years. For more than half an hour she luxuriated, ignoring any distracting thoughts of her work, her bills, her dirty house. She was not only feeling relaxed, she found herself waking up in ways she did not expect—*is sexuality part of awakening spirituality?*—and wondered what Tracy might have to say about *that*.

When the bath water went tepid and her drink was gone, Joan lifted herself from the tub, pulled the plug, and listened to the water as it gurgled down the drain. Feeling a need to cool down in more ways than one, she turned on a cold shower. That aroused her even more, almost uncomfortably. She finally dried off with an oversized Turkish towel, wrapped a terry-cloth robe around her body, turned the lights on, blew her hair dry, and crawled between the silk sheets she had splurged on—her forty-eighth birthday present to herself.

She set up her writing tray, pulled out some fine stationery, and began a note to Brother Theodore:

Dear Brother Theodore, she wrote in the beautiful script she didn't often have time to indulge in.

I have been thinking a lot about our meeting and our conversation last month. Tracy and I continue to talk now and then. She's becoming a true friend as well as a colleague. We've talked about my conversation with you, and she has listened and offered further insights. In fact, she keeps encouraging me to write to you. And I keep meaning to, but time seems to get away.

I have reread some T.S. Elliot. I've also started rereading Thomas Hardy's Return of the Native. *I've pulled out some of my own writing and enjoyed some, cringed over some. And I try to keep a journal, like you suggested. I don't do it every day, usually three or four times a week is all. But I guess it is better than nothing.*

I'm really thinking about how my soul had gone into hibernation and is now waking up. I feel like maybe my spiritual side has been sleeping. Or been drugged. Or on ice. Or dead even. I've worked so hard to push down my feelings and let my head be in charge. Now it's like that inner self won't be silenced anymore. But how do I access and nurture this awakening soul? I can feel it; I know it's there. But I don't know what to do about it.

Recently I've been thinking about my life—life after marriage and family. I'm beginning to feel that it's a bit shallow. My main goal in life has been prestige, power, and money. I have all those things now. But where has it left me?

In thinking about these things, I've decided I would like to accept your invitation to take a personal retreat at your monastery. January would be good—after Christmas and during the coldest part of the year. Can I come the third week of January?

I look forward to hearing from you.

Sincerely,
Joan Alexander

Joan stamped the envelope, put it with her purse and planner, and went to bed, feeling something like joy for the first time in ages.

**Chapter 8
Crisis**

It was almost 8:00 a week later. Joan had stopped for a bite to eat with Margaret after work. The red light on her phone indicated she had messages as usual. The first three were hang ups. Probably marketing calls. The fourth was Chip. His voice quavered. There was noise in the background. Where had she heard that noise before?

"Uh, Mom," Chip's voice sounded shaky. "Um, I'm in jail. I kind of got picked up for driving under the influence. Um, could you come down and bail me out? I mean, before 10:00 tonight? I really don't want to stay here overnight." He was almost in tears. "Um, please—bring $1,000 with you. I'll pay you back. Uh, bye." Joan held the receiver away from her ear and stared at it. "To delete this message, press seven," said the phone. She hung up.

Rage began to build. *What in the world has he done? Does he know what this could cost him? What if he can't go to law school now? What if he can't be a lawyer? Just bring over the $1,000. Like money grows on trees. And I'm just supposed to mosey down there and pick him up like he's a little kid at a friend's house. Am I glad I took my own car today; he might have been driving it. Fortunately that car was in his name!*

Even as these thoughts and the fury washed over her, Joan was on her way out the door, walking toward her car.

"Oh, Chip, Chip, Chip. You were doing so well," she cried aloud to no one in particular. Grief and rage took turns as tears streamed down her cheeks. *I'd better get ahold of myself or I'll get pulled over. No! No! No!* She unlocked and opened the car door, swung herself inside, and slammed the door behind her. Everything seemed to move in slow motion. She took a deep breath, blew her nose, and wiped her eyes, took another deep breath and started the car. This would be a night from hell. Thankfully, he was now responsible for himself. She and Charles would have no liability. And thankfully, no one had been hurt and nothing had been destroyed. *Just Chip's future*, she thought bitterly. *I wonder whether anyone would have kids if they knew how much it would complicate their lives. And it doesn't stop.*

Joan took the next day off, staying close to home. She did, of course, have her laptop and work in her briefcase. She had made arrangements for Chip's father to come this evening and talk to Chip. The house was clean so she didn't have to worry about that. But she was nervous about being with Charles. She was aware of lingering hurt. And though she was no longer "in love" with him, she was still drawn to him, fascinated by him even after the mess of their marriage. How would it all go?

Charles's new red BMW finally pulled into the driveway. Dry-mouthed, Joan met him at the door, trying not to meet his eyes or glance at the new wedding ring on his finger.

"Hello, Joan. This is really a shame, isn't it?"

"It sucks for sure." She let him in.

Joan led him to the den where a red-faced Chip was waiting, then left them alone for a while. From the kitchen she could hear the loud, strained exchange. After nearly an hour, the door to the den opened and a chastened Chip walked slowly up the stairs to his room.

"How'd it go?" Joan asked Charles.

"Well, you probably heard some of it. But basically, I told him what we agreed when you called today. That his future is his responsibility. That we are not going to bail him out again. That it's time for him to grow up. I told him he'd have to pay for his first year of grad school—whether he chooses to go ahead with law school or whether it's something else. If he proves himself the first year, we might help him out after that. We'll have to see how it goes. What will this do to his plans for law?"

Joan frowned inside her most professional demeanor. "It can't help at all."

"I'm not sure there's much more we can do. I'll be with you at the hearing. If you want me there that is. I'll be thinking about him, even if I'm not with you."

"Oh, that would be fine. I guess we're in this together in a way."

"I'm glad you feel that way." He paused, seemed a bit uncomfortable. "So, Joan. How are you doing?"

"Okay, I think. At least I was until this happened."

"Work going okay?"

"Yes, quite well in fact."

"Chip mentioned that there were some changes with you. That you'd been listening to jazz. Talked to an old monk about life or something." Charles's grin held a hint of mischief.

Joan smiled. "All true. I guess I'm at the age when I'm beginning to assess my life. Beginning to ask questions about whether I'm satisfied with where I've come."

"And are you?"

"Well," she looked him straight in the eye, summoning a courage she did not feel. "I wish my marriage could have been more successful."

"Yeah, well—"

"Sometimes I've wondered whether we'd have done it better if we'd paid more attention to the spiritual part of ourselves."

Charles guffawed. "This is not the woman I was married to for twenty-six years."

"Yeah, well, it's never too late to change I guess." Joan swallowed back a bit of embarrassment.

"Spiritual, huh? Like how do you mean?"

"Well, being more in tune with our inner selves, more aware of nature, more attentive to the inner needs of the kids, less driven, I guess."

"Midlife stuff. I guess I know something about that." He'd been looking at Joan but now looked away, then lowered his eyes and mumbled, "I guess life is never quite what we think it might be. Well, I'd better be going."

"It was good of you to come over, Charles. Thanks. Thanks for sharing this burden with Chip."

"Sure thing. He's my son, too. Always will be," and his voice cracked. He let himself out the door and was gone.

After he left Joan picked up the mail from yesterday and today that she had piled on an end table, then sat down to go through it. Her heart skipped a beat when she came to the envelope from Brother Theodore. She ripped it open and read:

Dear Joan:

It was very good to hear from you. I've been wondering about you, and I keep you in my prayers. I'm glad you have continued to think about your life.

The third week in January would be very good.

Enclosed is a form you should fill out and send back to me immediately, and we will get you set up for a weeklong retreat. I look forward to seeing you again.

Peace,
Brother Theodore

Margaret called Joan to her office. She wasn't Joan's immediate supervisor exactly, but had been Joan's mentor when she first arrived. And she was a senior partner. Margaret had been impressed with Joan's progress, dedication, comportment in the office, success, and quick climb to the top. But over the last weeks and months she had noted a change in Joan, a change that worried her. Why? Why did she care? Was it because she cared for Joan so much that she didn't want her to throw away her life? Well, there was that. She did care about Joan. She was happy about Joan's success for its own sake, but also because it reflected well on Margaret as her mentor.

Chapter 9
Conflict

She also cared about the firm. Joan was important to the partnership. She had been given important clients because of her ability and dedication and her innate people skills. She also took on the clients that needed a little extra TLC. Margaret was sometimes a bit envious of Joan's grace with people, but Margaret knew that she herself had a harder edge than Joan did, so she could take the cases that needed something other than an attorney with a heart.

But Joan was getting mushy, in Margaret's opinion. Margaret had even seen a few tears in the last several weeks. Not just once or twice. What was going on with Joan? She knew about Joan's friendship with Tracy. What they talked about, who knew, but Margaret bet they talked more than a little about religion. It was Tracy's "thing." Margaret liked Tracy but had less patience for Tracy's readiness to bring religion into everyday office talk. Tracy got away with more that she should, in Margaret's opinion, because she was so good at her work. She did everything she was told, did it well, then took the initiative to do more within appropriate bounds. She was helpful, courteous, kind, and very efficient. She was also very warm and personable, which was the part of her that made Margaret nervous. But why? Why was Margaret put off by that?

Margaret didn't usually think deeply about philosophical or metaphysical issues. She had rejected all of that when she was in college, deciding not to waste her life on something that couldn't be proved in more concrete ways.

Now Joan seemed to be going down that path, and something about it nagged at Margaret. She was irritated that Joan was making her reconsider those long-discarded ideas that she had successfully held at bay for many years—an insistent sense that there just might be something to religion and God, something Margaret just didn't want to deal with. She had worked so hard at controlling her feelings that she forgot they were there. She didn't like having them stir.

As Joan came toward the office, Margaret could see her through the window that opened out into the hall. There seemed to be a serenity about Joan these days. That unnerved Margaret too.

"Hi, Margaret. You called?" said Joan as she breezed into Margaret's office.

"Yeah, Joan. Sit down, please."

"Um, could we go to the lunchroom? I need a sandwich; I forgot to eat lunch. Could we talk there?"

"Sure," Margaret agreed, though she would rather talk in her office. In the elevator they exchanged a few words.

"How ya' doin', Margaret?"

"Oh, okay, I guess. Busy as always. Seems like I take work home every night so there's not much time for anything else. But that's what I've chosen, isn't it?" Margaret suggested pointedly.

"I guess most of us have." The elevator door opened, and the women walked into the lunchroom where Joan bought a tuna avocado sandwich on whole wheat bread with a Diet Coke. Margaret just had coffee. The room was empty except for one man sitting in the corner by himself. It was 2:00 after all. It would be an hour before many people would begin wandering in for coffee breaks. Joan and Margaret selected a table and sat down.

"What's up, Margaret?"

"Well, I noticed you are taking some time off in a week."

"Yes, I'm really excited! It's something I never dreamed I'd do. I'm going to take a one-week personal retreat at a monastery in California. Can you believe that? I met a monk a few months ago who invited me."

"Why on earth would you be doing something like that?"

"Oh, well—what's wrong Margaret? You seem upset."

"I'm not upset." Margaret never yelled, really. But the timbre of her voice deepened. "But I'm concerned about the change I have been seeing in you over the last few weeks, Joan. What in the world is happening? Ever since we got back from the cabin, something has come over you."

"I'm sorry Margaret. I didn't know anything about me was bothering you."

"Well, look—you're getting all mushy, for instance. I've seen you cry on the job more than once, for God's sake. You know that's questionable professionalism. I know you've been hanging around with Tracy. She's a nice person and all, but she's not cut out for the big time. I can't even see why you bother mentoring her. She won't ever be our kind of lawyer—her religion is too important to her. Is that what you two talk about at those long coffee meetings on Fridays?"

Shock registered on Joan's face. "Margaret, Tracy has been a real help to me. I've been troubled about some things, and Tracy has been a good advisor. The monastery thing has nothing at all to do with her. Something's been changing for me. Something spiritual."

"Well, I don't like how it's affecting your work."

"Affecting my work?" Joan managed a mirthless laugh. "Margaret, I've begun to feel a freedom inside that I have never experienced. And it frees me to be in better touch with my clients. I feel like I'm actually helping them, not just doing a job that gets them out of a pickle and fattens our coffers. I'm more satisfied with how I'm able to relate to my clients in caring about them, and not just about the facts of their case."

"That's what I'm talking about. This isn't a social service agency. This is an office of law, capital L, capital A, capital W. Your job isn't to care for people. It's to win cases. That's it. I hate to say it, but Joan, I'm afraid you are losing your cutting edge."

Joan mustered the glare that often made her so effective in the courtroom. "What you don't understand is that I feel like I'm just beginning to discover what is important and to connect with the humanity of my clients. They need much more than my legal expertise. They need some compassion. I had compassion before, but I usually didn't show it much. Now I realize they need me to show it."

"Like I said, Joan, this is not a social service agency. Your job is to give them legal advice and help them with their legal issues. Period."

Joan's voice was becoming more steely. "Margaret, I'm sorry to say that I disagree with you. I'm discovering some important things about myself and about life. I want to be true to those things."

"Joan, you're losing it. After all we've been through together, after all the support I gave you to help you succeed here at the firm—" Margaret broke off in disgust.

At that moment the firm's vice president walked into the lunchroom. He had obviously heard the last bit of the strained conversation and looked from Joan to Margaret, eyebrows raised in a quizzical, warning look. The women glanced at him.

"Well, I gotta get back," Joan said. "That Anderson brief needs to be finished by tomorrow. I'll be taking it home with me," she added pointedly.

"Good. I'm glad you have retained some of your professional standards," Margaret retorted, glancing meaningfully at the vice president who dispensed one last glance at the women before ordering.

After her exchange with Margaret, Joan explained the situation briefly to Tracy and let her know she was going home. She gathered her things and made an early exit. It was only 3:30 by the time she got out the door, but she had been at her desk since 6:30 that morning. She'd put in a day. She slipped on her coat, grabbed her briefcase, and walked out the door. She did not look into Margaret's office as she passed, though she did feel Margaret's eyes on her as she made her way past Margaret's open door and hall window.

In one way she didn't care. She knew her work would stand up to scrutiny. She was confident of that. Yes, she was taking more time for herself, but her work was still fine. Maybe better.

But Joan realized that Margaret was also her friend. That, for a change, was more important to her than the woman's position in the firm. It was something new. In the past, she had called herself Margaret's friend, but she had been more concerned with how that friendship could assist her own career. Today she recognized a sort of grief that Margaret was angry with her.

And it was true that Margaret could hurt her. Margaret was a tiger. In fact, some of the partners called her that—Tiger Lady. For some it was a term of affection and respect. For others, it was meant derogatorily. You didn't want to get on Margaret's wrong side. Once there, it seemed impossible to get back on her right side. Margaret was not very forgiving.

By the time Joan got home, she had a raging headache so she took a couple of extra-strength acetaminophen. She knew she had to finish the brief no matter what. As the medication began to work on her headache, Joan picked up her briefcase and spread her work on her dining table. Her worries about Margaret would have to wait. The Anderson brief could not. But Joan was aware that it was becoming harder and harder to dismiss her feelings and her growing sense of others. Still, Margaret would have to wait.

When the Monday morning came for Joan's trip to the monastery, Tracy drove her to the airport. Joan could have taken a limo or a taxi, but Tracy insisted. On the way to the airport, they stopped for lunch, Tracy's treat, and Tracy handed Joan a couple of small packages with a beautiful card. One of the gifts was a pretty book of lined paper for Joan to use as her journal at the retreat. The other was a box of elegant note cards. The note in Tracy's card was brief.

Dear Joan,

Wishing you the best kind of spiritual refreshment during your week in the desert. I will be praying for you. Feel free to write a note if you have a chance and the inclination—no obligation. I will look forward to hearing about your retreat.

Your friend,
Tracy

"Tracy, thank you. This is so sweet." Tears filled Joan's eyes. "I guess I'm getting a little emotional in my old age," she quipped.

"There's nothing wrong with that no matter what a certain senior partner might say about it," Tracy grinned. "Hey, we've gotta get going. Don't want you to miss your plane."

It was partly cloudy all across the Great Plains, but the sun flamed down on the cloud cover. Joan's thoughts meandered ahead to the unknown week she had begun. What exactly was she doing? What kind of a place was a monastery, anyway?

Chapter 10
Monday:
Transition

The flight attendant asked her beverage preference. *Do they serve any alcohol at the monastery? Maybe I'd better get a last glass of wine before I get off the plane.* She asked for a Chardonnay.

Then she pulled Tracy's note out of her purse and read its brief but soulful message again. Soon she fell asleep.

She woke with a jolt as the plane landed, confused by the remnants of a dream in which Brother Theodore had fetched her on a motorcycle. Her heart thumped wildly, and she had begun to perspire.

By the time the plane reached the terminal she had calmed down. Unusual for her, she waited for all the passengers to get out ahead of her and then took her small suitcase from the overhead bin. At the car rental, she noticed her hands shaking as she took the map and the keys from the indifferent rental agent.

She drove a long way before she began to feel the desert's loneliness. After she left the city, only a few structures lined her route. Ahead she was sure she saw Brother Theodore's monastery, a simple, three-story building, bringing her heart back into her throat as she considered anew the reason for her trip.

At the front desk she gave her name.

"Oh yes, we are expecting you, Joan." The fresh-faced young monk shook her hand. "We're so glad you are here. You are Brother Theodore's guest this week, is that right?"

"Yes. I am."

"Did you have a pleasant trip?"

"Yes, thanks."

"You're in room 210," he continued, explaining to Joan the directions to her room. "Here's your key. Do you need any help with luggage?"

"No thanks; this is all I have."

"When you've had time to freshen up a bit, Brother Theodore would like to see you. If you come back here to the desk, we'll tell you how to get to his office."

"Thank you. Thank you very much."

Joan headed for the double doors the receptionist had pointed out to her and went to the stairs. As she climbed she already felt warmth from the kind welcome she had just received. It was much more sincere than the cool and professional politeness of the hotels she was used to. The receptionist really seemed to be expecting her and to be sincere in his welcome.

The sparseness of her room took her aback: nothing on the pale walls but a plain wooden cross. A simple woven spread covered the single bed. Only a small closet, but it was enough for the few things she had brought. A small writing table and ladder backed chair hugged the only empty wall. The tiny bathroom had no tub, just a shower stall. At least she didn't have to share. *No long baths with jazz and White Russians this week!* That was okay. She could endure anything for a week.

She tested the bed, first pressing it with her hand, then sitting, then finally stretching out her long, lean body on it. She didn't realize till then how dry and tired her eyes felt. Closing them for just a moment she ordered herself to not to fall asleep.

Suddenly a bell sounded—long, rolling gongs, six of them. Joan didn't know where she was. It was dark. Across the small room on the desk she saw the luminescent dial of a small clock. 6:00, it said. Suddenly it all came back. *Oh, no. It's dinnertime. Where am I supposed to go?*

She answered a light knock at the door; it was the young monk from the front desk. "Brother Theodore is hoping you are all right. Did you fall asleep?"

"Yes. I'm so sorry. Where do I go for dinner?"

"Just down the stairs you took up, and to your right. If you are ready, I can show you."

"Well, I'm a little embarrassed. I never got around to freshening up after the flight."

"Dinner is only for forty-five minutes. Shall I tell Brother Theodore you will be there?"

"Yes, that would be great. Thank you. I'll hurry."

As Joan was putting the finishing touches on her makeup another knock came at the door. The receptionist again.

"Brother Theodore has asked you to meet him in his office. You can have a light supper with him. Here is a map of the building with his office marked—just downstairs, turn to your right, the fourth door on the left."

"Oh, thank you," said Joan.

She pulled the brush through her hair one more time and went out, locking her door behind her. She followed the directions to Brother Theodore's office and knocked on the door. Joan felt just the least bit nervous. She hadn't seen this man for four months, and had never met him before then. It was a little awkward. Brother Theodore opened the door, arresting her as back in the summer with penetrating blue eyes and white hair set off by his black cassock. The lines in his face seemed a bit deeper, but his smile was warm and welcoming.

"Welcome, Joan. I thought this would be a good time for us to catch up a bit. I'm glad you were able to get some rest."

"Oh, thanks. I'm a bit embarrassed."

"Don't be. You needed the rest, and supper is usually simple enough. Soup, salad, bread. Soup tonight is spicy carrot. Here, please sit."

Joan looked around the "suite." A door opposite the hall door opened into an office with a large desk and chair. In the front room she could see a stove top, sink, and cupboards along one wall, a love seat in front of a table holding two ivies and a lush fern, an ottoman, and an end table with a lamp and a few religious and psychology magazines. Next to the love seat was a Boston rocker. Around the room were more ferns and ivies, a rosemary plant, some cacti, and a huge jade plant. It was modest, comfortable, quiet. Brother Theodore's bookcase held a few volumes by Thomas Merton, an old monk she remembered from the sixties; a book on Thomas Aquinas; a book about saints.

From a pot on the stove top, Brother Theodore ladled soup into a bowl and set it with silverware wrapped in a napkin in front of Joan. Then he served himself. "When I saw you were not in the dining room, I decided we would eat together here." From a small refrigerator disguised as a cupboard, he took two fresh, heaping green salads and put them on the table. Then he took a long bottle from the refrigerator and two goblets from a cupboard. "Tonight I can add some Pinot Grigio to our supper." He poured the wine.

So I guess they serve wine here after all. I could have dispensed with the drink on the plane—and that weird motorcycle dream it conjured up.

"You're smiling, Joan. What is it?"

"Oh, nothing."

"Oh. Well, I'm so glad you are here. Have you had a chance to look at the folder they gave you when you got here? No? Well, I wanted to point out that prayers are not required of guests. The monks pray in the oratory here three times a day. Guests are more than welcome to participate if they like, but it is not required, nor necessarily recommended. It's completely up to you. When and if you do go to prayer, I think it would be wise for us to talk about your experience, that is if you'd like to.

"Thanks. Maybe later in the week."

"That's fine. I think it's a good idea to take things slowly." He smiled warmly and looked into her eyes. "How are you, Joan?"

"I'm fine, Brother Theodore. It's good to be here." There was a spark between them, Joan was sure. Not sexual, not romantic, but more like—how to describe it? Life force was the only phrase Joan could conjure. "You have so many plants. They are beautiful. I guess you take care of them yourself?"

"Oh, yes. One of the great pleasures in my life. Did I tell you I am a gardener?"

"No, did you?" She dipped her spoon into the soup. Roughly grated carrots mellowed in a smooth, creamy liquid and were spiced up just to Joan's tolerance. "Mmm. Very nice."

"Good. I hope it will be enough for you. Once in a while we find a reason for a feast, but generally we stick with simple fare. The cook takes out his creative urges on the wonderful soups he prepares."

He allowed Joan some quiet in which they both ate. After they'd finished their supper, Brother Theodore seemed to sense her exhaustion because he didn't press her to talk. But when he said good night, his face assumed a serious, teacherly aspect.

"Joan, I would like you to go back up to your room and spend some time thinking about what you expect to experience and learn here. Take some bread in case you get hungry later. Allow yourself to become rested. But begin to think about what you would like from this week. Maybe there are specific things you would like to talk to me about; maybe you'd just like to walk around and do some reading in our library. Whatever, please follow your inclinations. Maybe we could meet about 10:00 tomorrow? That will give you time for breakfast, and me time for prayers. If you don't want breakfast you can sleep in.

"Now, do you have anything you need to ask me or tell me?"

Joan thought. "No, I don't think so. I'm not thinking very clearly right now."

"That's fine. Jet lag. I'll see you at breakfast, then—maybe." He grinned.

Joan entered her room and closed the door behind her. How good to see Brother Theodore again in person. He made her feel so welcome, so valued.

Valued. Now why would that feel so good? Didn't she feel valued in her work? In her life? Joan walked over to the writing table. She sat down in the straight-backed chair and pulled a pen and spiral notebook out of her purse. *What do I expect to gain from this week away? Good question. Do I even know? Direction? Answers? Ways to unclutter my life?* What did she expect to get here?

"Rest," she wrote first, deciding to brainstorm for a while. "Relaxation. Unclutter life. Feel valuable. Feel good about myself. Examine my life."

The small clock in front of her read 8:50. Joan suddenly realized that would be 10:50 her time. She went to her sink for a glass of water and ate a piece of the grainy, delicious bread she'd saved from dinner. With crumbs still on her pillow, she decided to call it a day.

Out of the window she saw a beautiful green tree. Green except for a prominent branch halfway up that seemed stripped bare of foliage, gray-white in its deadness. The branch seemed to grow toward her, to reach out to her. It looked like an arm, bent at ragged, sharp angles, leafless, finger-like twigs beckoning to her. It grew oversized before her eyes, gnarled, twisted, dried up. Joan stood paralyzed by the window as the dead branch moved closer and closer to her. Just as it began to tap at the window, she found the strength to yell out— and woke up, perspiring heavily. The room was warm. She reminded herself that she often had weird dreams when she got too hot at night; was this an early menopausal symptom? To get her bearings Joan crawled out of bed and turned on the light. Only midnight. She still had most of the night ahead of her. She adjusted the thermostat and exchanged her fancy nightgown for an old T-shirt she'd stuffed in her bag at the last moment. Much better. Why she even bothered with nightgowns she didn't know. T-shirts were much more comfortable.

Before returning to bed, Joan decided to record her dream and talk to Brother Theodore about it. The dead branch. What did it mean? Why did it reach out to her? It had seemed so real, so menacing.

A loud, resonant gong woke Joan from the deep sleep she had finally fallen into after the strange dream. Disoriented, she frowned and looked around her. Pale light came in the window. She looked at the clock. 6:59. Just then her alarm rang. *Oh, yes. It's time for breakfast. I think I'll skip it. Get another couple hours of sleep.*

Unaccustomed as she was to sleeping late, and in unfamiliar surroundings, she couldn't get back to sleep. She got up, took a long shower, dried her hair, and dressed. It was only 8:15. Maybe she could at least get some coffee in the refectory.

Joan went down the back stairs and peeked through the slightly open door. A table with food and beverages lined the near end of the room. She stepped tentatively in and helped herself to some cooked cereal. Then she picked an orange and a banana out of a large bowl and poured herself coffee. There was quiet murmuring in the room, which was not as large as Joan would have thought, just a dozen round tables suited for about eight people each. One table was empty, others only partly full. She guessed the monastery was not at capacity this week.

"Good morning, Joan," a voice behind her said. Brother Theodore of course. "It's good to see you. Did you have a good rest?"

"It was fine, thanks."

"When we meet at 10:00, I'd like to show you around the monastery, but if you'd like you can walk around the grounds a bit beforehand. It's a nice day for it."

"Great."

"Please come sit with me. I'll introduce you to some people."

Joan took a seat, and Brother Theodore introduced her to people around the table. Most were monks from the abbey. Two were pilgrims like herself. The conversation remained general, talking about the desert, the irrigation project the monastery managed in order to grow its own vegetables, the weather. Thankfully, no one asked her any personal questions. Joan just ate, enjoying the coarse, ground wheat porridge and fruit. The coffee was too weak, though. *That's the trouble with being a connoisseur. You have a hard time with other people's coffee.* When she finished breakfast, without feeling compelled to speak to another soul, she followed the example of others, taking her dishes and silverware to the cart by the table and separating them appropriately. Then she walked outside as Brother Theodore had suggested. It was, indeed, a great day—so different from the deep freeze the Midwest was in now..

At 10:00 sharp she went down to the monk's office and found the door ajar. She knocked lightly.

"Come on in, Joan." He motioned her to the love seat while he took a place in the Boston rocker.

"So, did you think about what you would like to get out of your retreat here?"

Joan was unsure how to start. "Well, it's not terribly ambitious, but maybe a little rest, a little extra sleep."

"There's nothing at all wrong with that. Most people come here needing some rest before they can get on with anything else on their agenda."

"Well, I don't know if I really have an agenda."

"What is it you'd like to gain from your time here? Besides rest?"

Joan shared her list. "Relaxation. Learn to unclutter my life. Feel good about myself. Examine my life. Find out why I don't feel quite fulfilled in what I am doing . . ."

"That's a good list. First let me assure you, you won't solve everything here. You may not solve anything. But you can get started. You can learn how to think about life. You can allow that place inside, that soul, to live just a little more. You might find ways of opening more doors, and learning to let the breeze, so to speak, blow in, instead of always having it so stuffy inside."

"If I could get a good handle on what I might be missing, that would be good."

Brother Theodore chuckled. "Be patient. It will come. You'll notice that there will be a lot of quiet. You may even get antsy. No television. No radio. I don't suppose you brought a cell phone?"

"Uh, yeah, it's here." Joan patted her purse. "I thought I'd like to check back at work. And check on my son."

"Sure, check on your son. But I'd encourage you to resist checking up on things at work. A retreat is about getting *away*. About making space away from the ordinary. Just try it for as long as you can. A couple of days maybe. Then if you can't stand it any longer, make a quick call to Tracy or someone who can bring you up-to-date briefly. Who has your cell-phone number?"

"Just my son and Tracy. I got a new one before I came out."

"Well, I hope no one needs to get ahold of you."

Joan was suddenly steaming inside. *Who does he think he is to tell me what to do? Of course I need to connect with my office. That's who I am.* She almost didn't hear what Theodore was saying back to her.

"Why don't we take a tour of the monastery grounds? You are welcome to take a walk around any time. I'll just show you some places you might like to check out. Like our library." They left Theodore's office and walked down the hall, around the corner, and past the refectory. At the end of the hall was a large double door where tall shelves of books stood. Joan momentarily forgot her wave of anger and allowed herself to be awed by the size of the library, the number of volumes.

"Are these all religious books?"

"Not all are specifically religious. Most are related to spirituality in some way. Psychology for example." From the library they went out a back door and began to walk. Joan walked beside Brother Theodore in silence.

"You're very quiet, my friend. You seem a bit distant." Brother Theodore had a hint of a grin on his face and he arched his eyebrows.

"Oh. I just don't have anything to say, that's all."

"You wouldn't be just the slightest bit miffed that I would suggest you not contact your office?" Still that ever-so-slight grin.

"Oh." *How can he read my mind like that?* She averted her eyes. "I dunno. It does seem a little restrictive."

"Well, keep in mind, anything I suggest here is just that—a suggestion. If you really don't want to do something, don't do it. I'm just offering ideas that might help you get the most out of your week. It's a rather big adjustment, after all. In my experience, the more that people disengage from the ordinary in their lives, the more they are able to concentrate on what's inside. But it's up to you. Call Tracy as soon as we're finished walking if you need to."

Why am I so angry?

"Here is our inner courtyard, Joan. Most of our irrigation is for the purpose of growing food—fresh vegetables mostly. But we use some of the water to give us this lush refuge. It's one of our few luxuries. Why don't I leave you here for a while? As you now know, you can depend on the bells to inform you of what's next. At 11:30 they will signal midday prayers for the monks and other pilgrims who wish to pray together. The bell after that, at 12:30, will be for lunch. Sit here if you like. Go to your room. Walk around. Maybe think about why it irritated you for me to tell you not to call home. Or about anything you want. And try to rest. Inside and out."

"What do you mean?"

"Maybe that's something for you to think about. What does it mean to 'rest inside'? Would you like to get together this afternoon, say 3:00, and talk about it?"

Joan tried to squelch a burst of fury. "No! I mean, sure. What will we talk about?"

"Anything you want." Brother Theodore nodded. "Being mad at me! I need to go get ready for prayers. I'll see you at lunch?"

"Okay—of course."

How could she stand a week of this relaxed schedule? Or of this infallibly and insufferably kind man? She went up to her room and sat on the bed, her back against the wall, eyes closed. It was going to be a long five days.

Chapter 11
Tuesday: Change

Brother Theodore was engaged with several other people at lunch so Joan found a place by another woman during lunch at a table where there were at least as many pilgrims as there were monks. She listened to their innocuous conversation, but her mind was too jumbled to take part. After lunch, she strolled the grounds to get some fresh air and clear her head. She realized that her frustration with Brother Theodore was misplaced. Why did she turn on him? Fortunately, he was a good sport about it. Maybe he had a lot of experiences trying to "help" people. She sat on a stone bench and closed her eyes. A slight, warm breeze touched her face. A hot tear escaped one closed eye. Joan sniffed hard. Why had she agreed to come here anyway?

At 3:00, as scheduled, Joan appeared at Brother Theodore's office suite.

"Come in, Joan." As always, his ready smile. He handed her a cup of coffee. "Don't you like it black? And here, I have some cookies fresh from the refectory."

"Thank you." *How had he learned of her coffee tastes?*

"Did you get some rest?"

"Of a sort. I took a walk after lunch."

"I'm sorry we didn't get a chance to talk at lunch. It seemed you were well occupied."

"Yes. The others seemed like nice people."

"Good. What have you been thinking about since this morning? Anything you care to discuss?"

"Well, I'm afraid I was a little testy with you this morning. And I'm sorry about that."

Brother Theodore shrugged, unperturbed. "When you get into the business I am in, you get used to people taking their frustrations out on you."

"And what do you call your business?'"

"The formal name for it is spiritual direction. I'm what the church calls a spiritual director."

"So you're 'directing' me?" She emphasized "directing" with a snide tone of voice.

Theodore smiled into his cup of tea. "No, Joan. Relax. We would talk about it more formally were we to embark upon that very specific and special relationship we call spiritual direction."

"What does it mean, spiritual direction?"

"First of all, Joan, it's not manipulation, or control, or brainwashing, or bossing someone around."

"That's good to know."

"It sounds to me like you have an issue about people telling you what to do."

"I think a lot of women my age do. We've worked too hard to develop our expertise to tolerate not being respected. And I certainly don't like the idea of someone trying to control or manipulate me."

"That's healthy, of course. Have you had particularly bad experiences with that?"

"Oh, I don't know. Not any more than usual for a successful woman in the baby-boomer generation. I guess a lot of us grew resentful of our parents or professors—especially those who thought they were always right."

Brother Theodore got that piercing, serious look again. "One of the most important things a spiritual director can do is listen. And I can listen to anyone. I can ask questions. And listen some more. Perhaps as I listen to more of your story and to what you are experiencing here, I can offer you something that will be helpful to you in your quest."

Joan smiled. "You are a good listener, Brother Theodore. What sometimes unnerves me is that you seem to hear what I'm only thinking, what I haven't yet said."

He smiled and waved this away. "Experience, I guess. Have you thought any more about what you would like to get out of this week?"

"Not really. Maybe I should do some listening for a change. Maybe you have some wisdom to impart. Since I know now what you are up to, I think I am comfortable enough to allow you to guide me while I'm here. I feel like I've only begun the process of tending to my soul. You probably have some suggestions for me."

"Well, I do, of course. But I don't want to hurry things."

"Go ahead. I'm ready to listen."

"Right now I think it might be helpful to you if I described a continuum of psychospiritual progress. You see, I think that all of us are on a journey. The process of listening to our inner selves is just that—a process."

Brother Theodore stood and went into his office, coming back to the sitting room with a legal pad and a pencil. He scooted his chair around closer to Joan, sat down, and began writing on the tablet.

"Look at this. The first stage of psychospiritual development is what can be labeled as 'precontemplative.'" He wrote the word, then drew a square around it. He drew some arrows pointing to the square from all directions, explaining, "These are influences the precontemplative person is keeping out of his or her life."

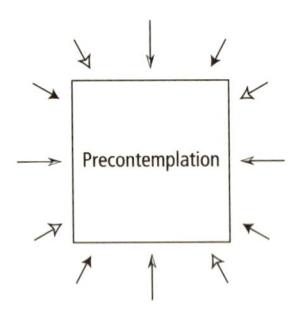

```
          ↘  ↓  ↙
        ↘ ┌─────────────┐ ↙
          │             │
       ──▶│Precontemplation│◀──
          │             │
        ↗ └─────────────┘ ↖
          ↗  ↑  ↖
```

Joan touched a few of the arrows with a forefinger. "What are these influences trying to get in?"

"I'll get to that. Now in this stage, people don't recognize any need for change or growth. And they are not open to any influences that might threaten their personal status quo.

"But everyone hits this stage; it's the starting point for any transformation."

He drew another neat square, then erased the corners and wrote another word inside it, drawing more arrows.

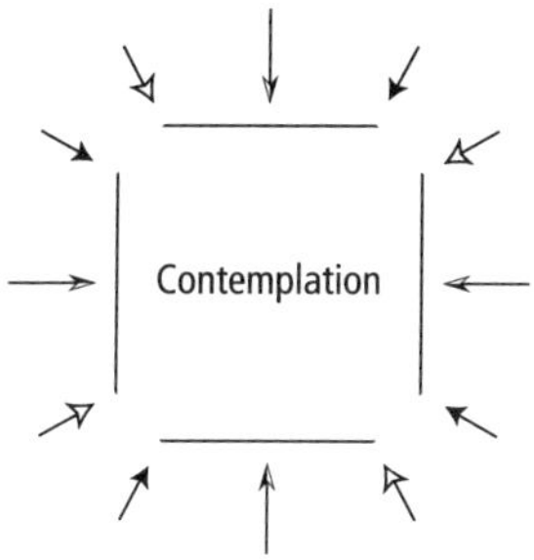

"The next stage is the 'contemplative' stage. Here people acknowledge that things are not perfect. Maybe first they backtrack and try to figure out how they got to this place in life. They struggle to understand the problems they seem suddenly aware of. They begin to think about possible solutions and become more open to influences and suggestions from outside.

"Following contemplation—" Brother Theodore drew a square with dotted lines, again writing a word inside—preparation. "This is when a person is serious about solutions.

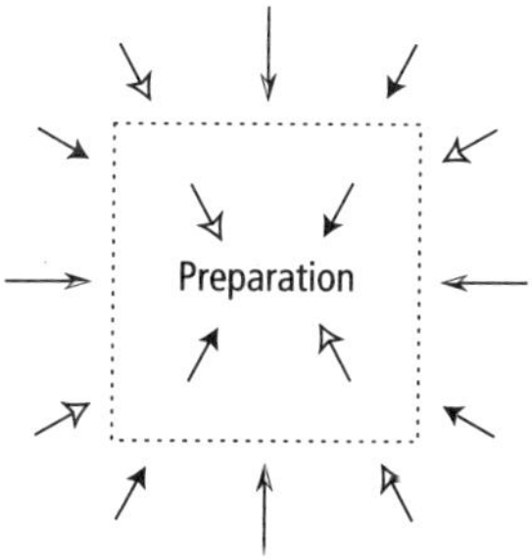

"People at this stage continue to reevaluate both themselves and their problems. They feel increasingly confident of their decision to change. They focus more on their future selves and less on their problematic past. In trying to learn from the past, they work to overcome their problems by finding suitable solutions. They become even more open to outside suggestions and outside assistance.

"Then there is 'action,' where the drive for change becomes manifest."

Brother Theodore sat back while Joan pored over the illustrations.

"There's also 'maintenance,' and 'recycling,' where you begin to start over again. But for now, I'd like to focus on the first three because, Joan, I think you are progressing beyond the precontemplative, but not quite yet at preparation. You may not be at preparation when you leave the monastery, and then again, you may be ready for some significant decisions about change. But it seems to me you have entered the contemplative stage. Do you understand where I am going with this?"

"I think so." Joan thought wonderingly about the last six months, distilled so aptly into Brother Theodore's paradigm. "It seems that maybe there was a breakthrough at the cabin last spring. Maybe my conversations with Tracy over the summer and going together to your lecture. Maybe asking you for that breakfast meeting was a movement from one stage to another—moving from where I obviously didn't see any need for me to change to a place where I would be a little more open to insights about my life."

"That's my impression, too. I would say that coming to the monastery marks a definite transition point, and that what you do here will be important in your spiritual development. We could call the process a spiritual journey."

"Some trip."

"Well, yes, sometimes the tough realizations seem like a big joke on us. But even those times can lead us to change and to maturity. In the contemplative stage, where I'd say you are now, you are beginning to try to understand some things in your life. You've at least acknowledged, if not a problem, a certain hunger or yearning. Would that be an accurate assessment?"

"Yes, I think so." Joan sipped her coffee. "Trying to think it through, evaluate what is bothering me, evaluate where I am in my life."

"Have you made any progress in that thinking?"

"A little, I guess. For so many years I've been so focused. I've achieved money, prestige, power. My parents are even proud of me, and believe me, they're very hard to please. Perhaps in my work I've helped some folks along the way, but it's been incidental. And where has it gotten me?" Joan opened her empty hands. "A failed marriage. Alienation from my kids. A life with few real friends. And a few good enemies." Joan paused. Her hands were loosely folded at the second joints of her fingers, the pose she often held when arguing a case, to make it look like she was just now thinking things through out loud. It was effective in helping a jury to think along with her, and to come to her conclusions. But now, she really was thinking out loud.

"The money, prestige, and power don't seem to satisfy me like I think they should. It seems like what I've lost is greater than what I've gained. Yet I worked so hard to gain what I have. It feels kind of empty inside. Like I need something more." She paused and looked at Brother Theodore, but he simply looked back at her, revealing nothing. She continued.

"I've become aware of the emptiness for some time over the last year. The empty bed, the too big closet, the house to myself. I've worked so hard to push down my inside feelings and let my head be in charge. But now it's like whatever is inside won't be silenced anymore." Joan swallowed back a knot in her throat.

Brother Theodore patted her hand. "Some of what you are experiencing is normal in our middle years. We reevaluate, realize we don't have forever on this earth, want very much to live significant lives. Some people begin to simplify a great deal. Some, particularly men, feel they've outgrown their current marriages and cut out of them, finding swinging singles lifestyles, buying sports cars."

"I know one of those men personally," Joan smirked.

Theodore smiled kindly.

"You know, Joan, you have been on your journey for many years, but you didn't know that. We aren't always aware of how we are changing. Sometimes we grow in a certain direction and discover that's not what we wanted after all. Then we begin to assess what it is we do want." The old monk finished his tea and set the cup aside.

"When you're aware that you are not satisfied, the next question follows easily: *What will satisfy me?*

"But getting and living the answers is a lifelong process. I don't have immediate answers for your questions. In fact, I don't have any answers at all. You will have to find those out for yourself. But I can assist you as you try to work it through."

Joan felt a small but thrilling dart of hope.

"Maybe one goal for this week is to try to assess the question, 'What might satisfy me?'"

"That sounds like a good start."

Brother Theodore stood up and brushed nonexistent crumbs from his clothing. "Perhaps you might ponder that before we meet this evening. I need to go to vespers now. And I want to reiterate that you are always welcome to attend those services. But you are not required. Maybe in the next couple of days you might just like to step in, to see what it is like. But no pressure. Would you like to meet again right after dinner?"

"Sure. I'll see you then."

Joan again walked the grounds, thinking hard about the conversation. *What would satisfy me? What would satisfy me? Am I really NOT happy? Or do I like my life but just need something more? Something new? What kind of something new would add the missing ingredient? I do help people sometimes. Isn't that satisfying? I've experienced a lot of loss lately. That could contribute to my sense of emptiness, of longing, couldn't it?.*

Joan found her way into a small courtyard where a fountain gently bubbled quietly in a corner, and a peaceful calm stole over her as she sat on a rough-hewn bench. The sun's heat and light dwindled. Underneath her busy barrister's identity, something indefinable began to stir, something just at the edge of her ability to comprehend. Memories long held at bay by her rational mind fought to be heard. How she had failed her family through the years, not in one big action or betrayal, but one incident at a time. She had shut them out, put them on hold, belittled them. Memories of how she had undermined her marriage in the way she sometimes talked to her husband—the "I'm right you're wrong" position she usually took in their disagreements. A tear rolled down her cheek and fell on her hands so carefully folded in her lap. It was the first time she had allowed pain to surface this clearly, this specifically.

Suddenly, Joan felt herself losing control of the tightly held dam of emotion. Terrified, she jumped up and half-walked, half-ran back to her room. Once there, she called her travel agent, anxious to get out of this place ASAP. No flights until Thursday afternoon. *Darn*. She then began to call her office to check on the progress of research preparatory for a trial starting in another month. Suddenly aware of how automatic her actions and work-focused mind took over, she hung up. *Cool it, Joan. Take a deep breath. You WILL stay. You WILL stay here just three-and-a-half more days. You can do it. It's not going to kill you. Probably won't even compromise your sanity. Not just three more days. Calm down.* Then with determination, she retraced her steps to the small garden, nearly dark by then, and sat herself down again. She folded her hands in her lap and closed her eyes. The most gripping of her feelings had lapsed during the abrupt run to her room, but she did begin to think deeply about some of her past that she regretted. *I've made mistakes. So has Charles. But I can only take on my own.*

So deep in thought, she jumped when the chimes announced dinner. Her seat in the little sanctuary was just beneath the bell tower. Joan laughed to herself, feeling somewhat more settled, walked inside, past the library and into the refectory.

As was beginning to seem usual, Brother Theodore was surrounded by others interested in talking with him. Joan sat at a table with a woman she learned was named Dianne, a therapist visiting the monastery to research psychospiritual development and to sit in on a seminar Brother Theodore and two other monks were giving. Joan wanted to be pleasant. "How is the seminar going?"

"Very well, thanks. And how are you, Joan? Did you have a pleasant afternoon?"

Ordinarily, Joan would have given an unrevealing reply. But what had she to lose?

"Up to a point. I started thinking about the change process Brother Theodore talked to me about. It started to get too intense and I panicked. Tried to schedule a flight out. I really wanted to bolt."

Dianne smiled. "You know, we sometimes do funny things on our way to change." It was a kind reply, but when Dianne turned right back to her food, Joan became wary. *Maybe she really doesn't want to get into it with me.* The rest of the table conversation was spent again on light topics.

After dinner, as planned, Joan met Brother Theodore in his office.

"Did you have a good afternoon, Joan?"

"I think so."

"You sound a little uncertain."

Joan hesitated. She wasn't about to tell on herself again. But his lined face was so appealing. "Well, I had a very strange dream." She told him about the tree with the dead branch that reached out to her. "Do you think it means anything?"

Theodore pondered this. "What do you think, Joan?"

"I'm not sure."

"Try talking about it."

"Something dead and sinister was reaching out to me." She hugged her shoulders and shuddered.

"What would a dead branch in a living tree signify?

"That there is some disease in the tree."

"Why would a dead branch be reaching out to you?"

"That's what I can't figure out."

"Do you think the tree could maybe be you?"

"How is it me?"

"Think about it."

Joan fidgeted with a tissue in her hand. Sighed. "Well, if the tree is me, then maybe the dead branch is something dead in me."

"Good. Go on."

"Well, maybe the tree has just started to be diseased in that place. Maybe it's the clutter in me, the deadwood that is urging me not to change. It doesn't want to be changed or discarded. Maybe it was some kind of subconscious entreaty to forget the growth process and stay with the deadwood in me."

"Good. Remember that you screamed out when the branch tried to reach you. That might indicate that you can choose change. You don't have to live with the old, hurtful ways. Maybe if you think along those lines you'll find some more clues. Perhaps it was just a dream. But you can attach some symbolism to it if that's helpful."

Joan's eyes shifted to her lap, to the shredded tissue in her hands. She suddenly felt vulnerable and a little afraid.

"It was so strange. So vivid. I woke up terrified. It took me a while to get back to sleep."

"Sounds like a proper nightmare." Brother Theodore was still for a few minutes, and Joan felt comforted by his presence and the quiet.

"Don't dwell too much on the sinister branch. Change is frightening. Even if we don't like some of the things in our lives, we're used to those things because they are familiar. We really can't see what change will bring us. I'm tied up tomorrow morning, but we could meet at 3:00 P.M. if that's okay with you?"

"Sure." Joan thought her voice sounded small.

"You have a lot to think about in the morning. You can stay in your room all morning, or go to the library, or sit out on the grounds. Sometimes I do my best thinking when I'm walking around. Would you like some suggestions for your reflections?"

"I would—very much."

"Try writing some thoughts down about change, and about being here at the monastery. About what you've observed here. How you feel about the rhythms of the monastery. Perhaps even about how you react to me. You don't have to share anything you write. Only if you want to. Do you think that will be enough to keep you going until 3:00?"

"Oh, I think so. I have some thoughts of my own that keep creeping up. I don't think I'll have trouble staying occupied. Did I tell you Tracy gave me a journal to keep notes in while I was gone? I've been jotting some things down in there. So I'll write, but it won't be a law brief."

"Sounds like a plan. Good night for now, my friend. Sleep well. See you tomorrow."

After she had left, Brother Theodore sat at the table across from the crucifix on the wall. He folded his hands and rested his head on them. He was convinced that this woman was truly on a spiritual journey, that God was drawing her to himself, and that in time she would embrace a life with God at it's center. He would not even try to venture a guess as to how long that would take, but he was quite certain that it would happen in time.

He truly believed that God had entrusted her soul to his care, and he was at once humbled by and fearful of that. Though through the years many had come to him for spiritual guidance, he never took their trust for granted. He had learned not to let his popularity as a spiritual director go to his head. Too many failures had taught him humility. His life of wandering away from God had taught him how far away he himself could stray.

As he thought about Joan, he began to lift her up to God in prayer. "Lead her by your love, toward your peace and hope. Give her evidence tonight that you are good and the lover of her soul. Let her rest in a peace that somehow, deep down, assures her of your love and care for her. In the name of the Father, and the Son, and the Holy Spirit, Amen."

The old man was tired, but it was a good fatigue. His greatest reward in all the world was to help seeking souls begin to find their center in God. Joan was on her way. He sighed a contented sigh.

On Wednesday Joan woke up again to the beautiful chants of matins. They were nothing like the hymns she'd dutifully sung in Sunday school, and yet they were strangely familiar. She decided to visit morning prayers before she left on Saturday.

After breakfast Joan took a walk around the monastery grounds and then met Brother Theodore at 3:00 A.M. as planned.

Chapter 12
Wednesday: Seven Smooth Stones

"Good morning." He started right in. "Joan, I have an assignment for you for your free time this afternoon. But first, let me tell you another story." He said,

Once upon a time, a long time ago in a little town everyone was ill, angry, not speaking to neighbors, because of a feud a long time before. Anger kept the sun from coming through to the town. The city council decided something was very wrong and asked a monk from a nearby monastery to come to town. The old monk had been on assignments of this kind before. Before traveling to the town, he prayed St. Patrick's breastplate prayer against all evils, invoking the strength and power of Christ as he went on his way. Then he headed for the little town.

When he got there he was amazed to see all the anger that polluted the little town and kept the sun from shining through the gloomy clouds. He talked to the members of the town council, and he met with the elders of the town. He talked with the women who drew water from the well. After observing for a few days, he gathered the people into a town meeting. He led them outside the town, where the cloud of gloom lifted. He showed them the green grass, the flowers, the tall, shady trees. They'd lived so long without these that they had no idea what they were missing. They thought their town was normal.

On the second day, the monk gathered the townsfolk together and took them to a creek where the water was cool and sweet and clear. On the creek bed were smooth stones. He instructed each of them to take one stone from the creek, just big enough to wrap their hand around.

On the third day, he instructed them to gather the vegetables from their garden and to bring their best spices. Everyone laid their offerings at the monk's feet by midmorning and went on about their daily chores, with instructions to return for the evening meal. After they left he began to cut up the onions, potatoes, carrots, leeks, celery, and tomatoes, and to mix them together in a huge pot. Midway through the afternoon he built a fire under the pot. As the vegetables cooked down, he added spices. By late afternoon, a delicious aroma permeated the air of the village.

While the delectable mixture cooked, the monk began to look for pieces of pottery, which he found here and there on the outskirts of town. He chiseled holes into several items, strung them on a green branch he had bent into a circle and tied, and hung it from a tree. The wind began to cling the pottery together, making music.

When the villagers arrived for their evening meal, the monk ordered the council members to serve a bowl of soup to every two people. Each villager had to share a bowl of soup with one other person in the village. The monk told them to speak to each other only of good things.

The villagers obeyed, some with great reluctance. But soon an amazing thing began to happen. They began to confess with tears the anger and jealousy and hatred that had weighed them down. As the anger left their souls and their bodies, the clouds above began to separate, and golden sunlight streamed through. A light breeze began to blow, and they heard the crude music of the chimes. The monk withdrew a small flute from his vest pocket and began to play.

The more they ate, the happier they felt. The old monk began to dance. He danced and danced. And the people began to dance with him. They danced far into the night.

The next day, the old monk reminded them of the stones they had collected. They would serve as a memory of this day when antique offenses and age-old hatreds were disbursed, and music flourished again, and friendships waxed, and the sun shone, and the grass grew green and the trees tall and full. Whenever the villagers felt frightened or angry, they clutched their smooth stones and remembered the monk's advice and counsel.

Brother Theodore ignored Joan's puzzled expression. "Joan, you can draw the parallels to your own experience as you will. You may discover insights from this story later on. Think of it like another dream, like the frightening one you had about the dead branches. In the meantime your assignment this afternoon is to go to a little creek on the outskirts of the monastery grounds. Here's a map. When you get there, look for seven smooth stones in and around the creek bed."

"Why seven?"

"You'll see." His eyes twinkled playfully as he grinned at her. "It's a surprise."

"How big should they be?"

"Just large enough to hold comfortably in your closed hand, like in the story. And here's a bag you can put them in."

After lunch, Joan did go to the little creek. She walked briskly, but not so fast that she couldn't savor the fresh air, the gentle warm breeze blowing off the desert, the low vegetation growing around her. A jackrabbit scampered across her path, startling her, reminding her of the weekend at the faraway Wisconsin cabin. She clutched the canvas bag that Brother Theodore had given her.

When she reached the creek, she took off her shoes and went wading. That was really all she could do with the amount of water in the stream. The first stone sparkled with rose tints, and she picked it up and rolled it around in her hand. The sun warmed her back pleasantly. A little perspiration gathered on her brow as she gathered another smooth stone, a black one, then another, this one alabaster white. Each stone resembled the others in size but had its own unique shape. She wondered why Brother Theodore wanted her to gather seven stones. One would be sufficient to remind her of the monastery. Nevertheless, she took her stones back to her room. Then she picked up her journal and went outside to the little garden.

> *I've been here two days now. Yesterday I wanted to bolt. Today I feel like I'm getting used to the special rhythm of the monastery, the quiet, the peacefulness. For the first time I feel like it might be hard to go back to the real world.*
>
> *Brother Theodore is amazing. He seems to read my mind sometimes and not be offended by what's there. It almost makes me feel like there could be a loving God. This is all very strange and new. So different from anything I have ever experienced.*

> *We talked about change. I need to think about the labels he gave the different steps of change. He called me 'contemplative.'*
>
> *My emotions seem nearer the surface than they've been since I was separated from Charles. But these emotions are not the angry-full-of-rage-and-self-pity emotions of almost three years ago. The tears are cleansing somehow. The emotions are different from anything I've known before. They come when I'm deeply touched by something. When I feel cared for. When I begin to remember things in the past that I am sorry for. When I think of how I would like to change things in the past.*
>
> *I should ask Brother Theodore what to do about those things I can't change and am beginning to feel so bad about.*

Then the chimes called worshipers to vespers.

Joan stood tentatively outside the oratory listening to the beautiful chants, allowing the music to wash over her, the spoken words of Scripture to soothe her. She did not concentrate on the words or the exact meaning, just let the sounds surround and comfort her.

"Come on in," said a voice behind her. The tall, bespectacled monk held the door and beckoned her through it. Joan felt too awkward to refuse. The monk handed her the Psalter and went on in ahead of her. He left her behind as he took his place among the other worshipers.

Joan slipped into the back row of chairs; there were only five rows so it didn't much matter, but at least it gave her the chance to sneak out if she wanted to. She did not open the book. She just stood with her eyes closed. Before she knew it, she heard the sounds of the meeting breaking up. Books snapped shut, and worshipers got to their feet. She opened her eyes. From the front row Brother Theodore smiled at her. Joan returned his smile. She waited in her place until he got to her, and they walked out together.

"It's good to see you here, Joan."

"Yes, well, I didn't intend to come in, but I did and I'm glad. It's beautiful."

"I'm glad you liked it. Shall we sit together at dinner tonight? A couple of others will be sitting with me, but you are most welcome to join us."

"Thank you; that sounds good."

Though Joan sat at Brother Theodore's table, she really didn't have much chance to speak with him until they met afterward. She again knocked gently on his door bearing her bag of stones and heard his warm "Come on in." When she entered the room, the lights were a bit dimmed, and there was a single candle on the table. He took her bag of stones. The music on the stereo was—what was it? Chants. She could imagine monks filing into their cathedral singing those songs of praise. Though they'd just had dinner, Brother Theodore offered Joan some tea. When they'd both sat down he closed his eyes, as if listening to the music, or sleeping, or even dozing off. He said nothing, unlike the previous times she'd come to see him. The silence with the music stretched out. Finally she ventured, "I've never heard that music. What is it?"

"Come to the quiet." Brother Theodore replied without opening his eyes or changing his position. More silence. Minutes seemed to stretch into hours.

"Why the candle?" she ventured again. "Is something wrong?"

"Shhh. Listen to the quiet."

Joan put her slightly cold hands around the warm teacup and closed her eyes.

After many long moments, Theodore opened his eyes and looked over at Joan. "What did you feel during the vesper service, Joan?"

An old, childhood memory suddenly surfaced. She was a little girl, seven or eight, and the family had gone to her grandfather's funeral. She had been intrigued by what the minister wore (she didn't know to call him a priest) and the various other accoutrements of the church. Her own church did not have the same kind of beautiful windows, the smoking, funny-smelling stuff and bells. Her own pastor did not wear such fancy things, and the choir sounded very different. Her own church didn't have the same kind of service at all. Of course, this was a funeral. Maybe everyone had the same funerals. When she got home she began to ask her father about the service. He brushed her off, saying they didn't mean anything, that Grandpa had "changed religions" when he married this grandma, after her first grandma died. That it was just a different way of doing religion. She had thought maybe she had asked a bad question, so she never brought it up again. It had sunk to the abyss of her consciousness until just now. As she explained this memory to Theodore, she said, "I guess there was a certain curiosity. I don't know if it was just a child's wonder or whether there was more. It's funny how that just now came back to me."

"Hibernation. Remember? You have to have been awake in order to go into hibernation."

Joan considered that. "You mean that was evidence of being awake spiritually?"

"Well, I think it was a combination of childhood curiosity and the openness that children naturally have toward spiritual things. Children are really open to just about anything. Very impressionable. Unfortunately the spiritual awareness they have, the spiritual openness, the wonder and awe is too often squeezed out of them. It takes the will and the space to help it come back."

Joan felt for the first time that someone could look through her and not judge her, not weigh her innocence or guilt. Could be totally accepting and affirming. She almost believed that things could be better and life could have deeper purpose and meaning.

Yet when she considered the logical, sequential lawyer-type thinking and rhythms she knew, she realized change would not be easy. She came back to the present with a sarcastic response.

"Brother Theodore, you almost had me going there. The candle, the tea . . . oh, you're good. Now," she leaned forward. "What about those silly seven stones? The surprise?"

The old monk smiled knowingly. "How easy it is to be distracted from the inner life."

"Huh?"

"Never mind. We can talk about it later. I wasn't just teasing you, Joan. I was testing your comfort with silence, your comfort with going a little deeper. And you did. Just a little. St. Isaac the Syrian said: 'Speech is the organ of this present world. Silence is a mystery of the world to come.'"

"Hmmm." Joan watched the candle.

"Even your embrace of silence, Joan, is a sign that change is occurring."

Joan just looked at him. *What about those silly stones?*

"Why don't we leave it there for this evening. Tomorrow I will not be available until 3:00. Spend the day thinking about the change process. Decide where you are on that continuum. Where you would like to go. Think about what areas of your life need healing. Maybe write in your journal some more."

After Joan left, Brother Theodore arranged the stones around the candle and prayed over them. "Lord, please hallow these stones so they can be a special means of grace for Joan. As she holds each one, help her to feel the power of your spirit and the strength that she will find in each discipline. Let her know that you are the God with the power to change her life. In the name of the Father, and of the Son, and of the Holy Spirit. Amen."

Chapter 13
Thursday: Regret and Forgiveness

Joan had taken some fruit from the refectory yesterday and decided to stay in her room for the first part of the morning. She wasn't hiding out exactly—she just wanted to think and write in her journal. When the chants wafted up the back stairs to her room, Joan tried to concentrate on their beauty, their peacefulness, entering into the idea that these sounds were actually lifting up to God in heaven, or wherever he was. When the chants ceased, she opened her eyes and faced her journal. She felt self-conscious about the few things she had written. Some of it reflected the legalese she was so used to. She was quite sure a personal journal shouldn't sound like this. So she had tried to write as if she were writing a letter to someone, or just talking out loud, Still it felt odd. Childish. Self-centered. But then, her journal was supposed to be about her. She began to write again.

> *I've been here almost three days now. I'm beginning to get used to it, I think. I feel protected. I didn't know I felt unsafe. Maybe vulnerable is a better word.*
>
> *It is so quiet here. People are busy downstairs in the offices, but you rarely hear a sound up here. Sometimes people passing by, or greeting each other. And the cleaning people are out in the halls just now, cheerfully working away. I*

can't understand what they are saying, since they are speaking in Spanish. But they seem quite happy in their work.

I'm not sorry that I went into law. It's been a good place for me in many ways. It uses many of my talents. But in the process of doing my best there, I lost a lot of opportunities to make sure my marriage was okay. Lost opportunities to secure my relationship with Charles. Lost opportunities to bond with my children. I guess I always thought I was missing something but kept thinking that next week, next month, next spring or summer there would be more time. And now my career is about all I have left. It no longer seems like enough. I guess I've spent more time with Tracy in the past few months than I have with anyone for a long time. Fun time. Relaxing time. My friendship with Tracy has made me realize how much I long for relationships. How much I've pushed them out of my life to succeed in law.

I can't believe that I'm beginning to see that my success in law is not enough for me. I'm beginning to regret how I've made my family second to law. I wonder if Brother Theodore has anything to say about how to heal regret?"

There she stopped, exhausted from the concentration. She decided to take a shower and get dressed. She stood under the warm stream for a long time, taking comfort in the heat, the water, the calm. Finally she dressed and went outside, leaving her hair to dry on its own as she walked the monastery grounds.

At lunch she sat by Dianne again. Though she didn't want to impose on Dianne's professional expertise, Joan wished she could ask the therapist about the psychological upheavals Joan was experiencing. Instead, she asked her how the seminar was going.

Dianne was eager to reply. "Oh, it's really going well. The three monks that do it are really good. They all have psychology degrees as well as degrees in other things that relate to spiritual and psychological growth. I always feel like I grow personally myself, though the reason for being here is totally professional."

"Do you feel like your professional life and your personal life relate?"

"Well, sure. I mean, I spend so much time in my professional life that if my person wasn't there I would be lost. In psychotherapy, if you aren't there for your clients, you aren't being authentic as a resource for people."

"Do you have any regrets about choosing psychology and being successful in your career?" Joan felt herself listen all over her body for the answer.

"No regrets about choosing psychoanalysis as a career. My regrets have to do more with my life outside the workplace. I missed a lot with my family. I was lucky to have a husband who had more flexible hours so he could arrange his time around the kids. We traded off time when they were little. He would work during the day, and I would take nighttime and weekend appointments. As the kids grew up, I took more and more clients and spent more and more of my time away from home, until I was hardly seeing them at all."

"Sounds a little bit like me. How is your family now?"

Dianne gave Joan a rueful smile.

"Well, let's just say the kids have all learned to live without me. I'm lucky that my husband cared enough about our relationship to hang in there with me, but we've got a lot of healing to do. I hardly know my kids. He's the one who knows them. He's the one they come to in crisis. The kids are pretty angry with me about my absence in their lives."

Her life is a lot like mine. But I would never expose it the way she is. That takes courage. Then she said, "You're so open about your regrets. That takes a lot of courage."

Dianne responded, "If I tell my clients to be open and honest about their issues, I guess I should follow suit, huh? Anyway I'm not this open with everyone. I tend to be freer here where people don't know me."

"Your life is a little like mine. Except I'm in law. Do you ever get over the regret in your life?"

"Well, I haven't yet. I guess I'll never totally get over it. Instead, I've reached a place of self-forgiveness. That doesn't mean I excuse myself for those things, but I don't beat myself up about it anymore. It's part of my past. I'm sorry. I still shed tears over some of it sometimes. But I've moved on. My husband has been great. I'm so thankful that he was there for the kids. That they had someone around when they were teenagers and in college."

"Is your family pretty much grown up now?"

"Oh, yes. One still in college but a senior. One married and in grad school. One just presented me with my first granddaughter."

"Wow, how nice."

"Yes it is, very. I love her a lot. Her name is Jenna." Then, like any doting grandmother she pulled out a picture.

"Oh, how sweet," Joan murmured, touched by the new grandmothers openness. Would Brad or Alison, or even scattered young Chip, one day make her a grandmother, too? And would she find the time to be a real grandma?

Dianne tucked her picture back in her billfold. "Joan, I don't know you or why you are here, and it isn't my business, but I just want you to know, for what it's worth, that it is possible to move on from your mistakes in life, to heal from the hard things. Of course, you can't ever turn the pages back, but you can learn from your mistakes. You can help others learn from your mistakes. There is life after failure. And there is healing and wholeness. I'm just guessing you wouldn't be here if you weren't looking for something. But I just want to encourage you that wherever you are, there is life beyond that place, and it is worth reaching for. And you can learn to forgive yourself. " Abruptly, Dianne looked away and covered her mouth.

"Sorry, I didn't mean to preach to you."

"Not at all." And Joan, usually so protective of her privacy, meant it.

Dianne stood and adjusted her skirt. "I'm sorry. I have to run. I'll be late for my next class."

After she left, Joan cleared her dishes. She wandered outside once again. *Wow. I guess I'm not alone. I guess I'm not the only one who screws up. How timely, what she said. Almost like it had been planned. She could be another soulmate, like Tracy, if we lived near each other. I wonder where she does live?* Savoring the stillness she hiked a little further than she had before, taking a path that led to a large outcropping of rocks. Joan skirted around the formation, savoring the sage-spicy air and the austerity of cactus and pale rock. A couple of lizards skittered across her path. A saucy, jay-like bird lifted from the top of the rocks and flew away from her.

As she walked, Joan found herself envying Dianne for her caring husband who had stayed with her in spite of their difficulties. A feeling of deep resentment, and then something else. A feeling of sorrow that Charles had left. Sorrow for what they had missed together. Sorrow for what she would never experience with her kids. A sense of utter loneliness. Even self-loathing. *Will I ever be able to forgive myself?* She turned and walked back to the little garden, chose a stone bench against the wall, and sat, pressing her back and head against the firmness of the building. This time, instead of trying to stuff the emotion down, she let the tears fall. She let soft sobs shake her for a few minutes. When the emotion spent itself, she blew her nose and wiped her eyes, surprised by the strange, new calm that settled on her in the tears' wake. She would have to talk to Brother Theodore about this. She looked at her watch and quickly left the pleasant cove in order to keep her afternoon appointment.

She reached his door and knocked more boldly than she had before.

"Come in," Brother Theodore called. "Good afternoon. It's

teatime again, Joan. You can take me out of Ireland, but you can't take Ireland out of me." He poured her a cup of good, strong tea. "Here, have some cookies—almond biscotti, I believe. Well, are you having a good afternoon?"

"Let's say it's been thought provoking."

"Would you like to talk about it?"

"I have to admit, having so much time to think gets to me."

"How do you mean?"

"Well, I think about the mistakes I've made with my family. With my husband in our marriage. Things I won't ever be able to make up. This noon I talked with Dianne, the therapist who's in your seminar." Brother Theodore nodded. "Her life is pretty similar to mine in some ways. We talked about regrets."

"What did she say?"

"She said you can learn to forgive yourself. What a concept. She said the regret doesn't ever really go away, but you learn to live with it. But I'm not sure I can ever forgive myself. And the prospect of living with the regret the rest of my life really hurts. Can I ever make up to my children what they lost by having a mother who was totally wrapped up in her job?" Just having the grizzled monk's attention soothed Joan from the inside out.

"Good questions, Joan. Again, I probably can't give you answers that will satisfy you. But I do agree with Dianne, that you can learn to forgive yourself. When you learn from your mistakes, you can move on to a rich and rewarding life. You can learn to live with your losses, accept them as part of who you are *today*. Remember my Chicago lecture about inner clutter? The sadness you feel now, the deep regret, are part of the clutter in your life. But those regrets and other deep, heavy feelings can be transformed into lessons that take you to a new place in life. You may never get over the regret and the wish that you could change things. But you can come to appreciate that those feelings led you to what is really important in life, giving you a chance to change before life is over. You can never turn the clock back, but you can work at healing your relationships with your kids where you and they are now. And maybe in the process, show them what is really important in life."

"Hmm." Joan was quiet for a moment, willing her surging, deep emotion to recede. Finally, she ventured a question that had been on her mind since last fall when she first heard Brother Theodore talk.

"Brother Theodore, when you spoke last fall about Granné and your daughter, Rea, there was obviously deep emotion there. You recall them with such pleasure. Yet it was obvious that you still miss them. How do you cope now with that loss? I hope I'm not being too presumptuous in asking that question."

The monk practically seemed to open like a flower. "Not at all. I'm happy to talk to you about it. In fact, I'm glad you asked. You see, one of the things I don't really emphasize in my talks—it would make them too long and distract from the points I'm trying to make—is that Granné was a very devout Celtic Christian. That was one of her characteristics that charmed me. God was very real to her. I went to mass every week, and to confession, and participated in Eucharist. But there was something more about Granné's faith than just those things. She truly believed in a loving God. She truly believed grace was dispensed in receiving the sacraments. As a Celtic Christian she had a prayer for every routine in her life. For example, she prayed a special prayer for fixing coffee in the morning. She prayed, 'As I fix this coffee to warm and waken our bodies, Spirit of the Three, descend on me to warm and waken my soul.' Then she would cross herself. I didn't know she did that for a long time because I usually wasn't in the kitchen yet. But one morning I caught her. She was just crossing herself, and I wondered whether something was wrong. It amused me when she told me about her prayer. But she was so serious about it. It was part of her life."

Brother Theodore wrung and unwrung his hands. "The pain of missing Granné and Rea is always there. Not one day goes by when I don't think of them. I sometimes talk to Granné. I don't know if she hears me, but I talk to her anyway. I say, 'Granné, I'm naming this rose for you.' I've learned over time that God's grace heals, but that I have to be open to the ways God chooses to shows me that grace."

A smile played on his mouth as he gazed out the window. "Sometimes when I'm walking in the afternoon, I think about her and my loss of her. And I have to truly say today that I am thankful—yes, thankful!—for all those hurts. Because if it weren't for those losses, I wouldn't be here now. It might have gone easier for me if I hadn't reacted the way I did. Instead of bringing God my anger and pain, I took it with me as I walked away from him, and it became a heavy burden. I tried to erase the pain in very destructive ways, as I explained at the lecture. But my response to God merely revealed that my relationship with him and my practice of my faith was not as strong or as real as I had thought. Still, in all my wandering, God was there. I didn't know it then, but I see it clearly now. God was there, waiting to take me home.

"So today when I walk, I sometimes thank Granné for leaving, so I could join her in that depth of soul. I think she must have prayed for me a lot. I think she still prays for me. I think that's one reason I am here today. Without her, I wouldn't have the opportunity to help others down the road to healing and faith."

Joan was very quiet, looking at the crucifix across the room full on for the first time. Deep inside something stirred. Awe. Humility. The room rang with quiet. She wasn't quite sure what to do with what he had said, but she knew she'd been given a great gift. The trusty chimes rang for vespers.

"I have to go now. I don't know whether what I've said helps at all."

"Oh, yes. Thank you so much. I'm not sure I should have asked. It was really quite personal. But I'm grateful that you told me."

"Not at all. I'm glad you asked. See you after dinner?"

"Yes."

The warm, inner light glowed from Brother Theodore's office Wednesday evening, the door slightly ajar. Joan knocked gently and pushed the door open at the same time.

"Hello," she said softly. Brother Theodore stood from his place in the Boston rocker. He was still such a tall, imposing man, for all his years.

"Hello, Joan, welcome again. Please sit down."

She took her usual place on the love seat.

"Joan, you told me your dream about the dead branch. It reminded me of another 'branch' story." He said,

Once there was a young girl who worked in a garden. She loved the feel of the dirt in her hands, loved to tromp in new spring mud in her bare feet. She loved the smell of the wet earth when she worked. She loved the seasons that visited the earth. She loved the kiss of the winter frost and the warm, sweet breath of spring. She even loved the heavy, hot, long days of summer. In the autumn, her garden was covered with a blanket of leaves, then winter covered over that with deep, white snow. When spring came, the little garden would be dressed in beautiful flowers.

The pride of her garden was a grapevine she had once planted. She had rescued it one day when she passed a grape vineyard and noticed it discarded during a farmer's pruning.

The little girl planted the vine and cared for it and watched it grow thick. Branches from the vine brought forth wonderful grapes. Her small field produced the best grapes around. One day a man new to town wandered past her garden. He stopped when he saw her grapevine and asked if he could try one of the grapes. The grapes were dark and full of luscious juice. He told her the grapes were the best he had ever tasted.

"What's the secret to your good grapes?" he asked her.

"Oh, sir, it's in the vine. I water it. I nurture it. I let the plant get plenty of sunshine. Every year I wrap it up against the cold during the winter."

The stranger looked at her with warm and gentle eyes. He said, "You are so right about that. It is in the vine." Then he walked on.

"Joan, this story recalls one that Jesus told his disciples. It comes from the Bible, and I'm reading to you in a new version that sounds like today's everyday English.

> *I am the Real Vine and my Father is the Farmer. He cuts off every branch of me that doesn't bear grapes. And every branch that is grape-bearing he prunes back so it will bear even more. You are already pruned back by the message I have spoken.*
>
> *Live in me. Make your home in me just as I do in you. In the same way that a branch can't bear grapes by itself, but only by being joined to the vine, you can't bear fruit unless you are joined with me.*
>
> *I am the Vine, you are the branches. When you're joined with me and I with you, the relation intimate and organic, the harvest is sure to be abundant.* John 15:1-5, The Message

"You see, this branch story is like a picture of the relationship we can have with God. And you are beginning to discover it. God is the gardener. If a branch isn't growing grapes, he cuts it away from the vine so it won't take energy from productive branches. But if a branch shows signs of growth, and bears grapes, he nourishes it, prunes it, provides it with opportunity to grow and produce fruit. I think it's evident, Joan, that you are a branch with a tendency toward life. That the Great Gardener is giving you the chance to grow."

Joan wondered about what this really meant. A lawyer—becoming a Christian? Praying on a regular basis? She remembered Margaret's scathing assessment of Tracy's faith.

Brother Theodore let Joan brood. "Joan, you've done some good soul-work today. And that's the hardest kind of work. I'm going to let you go. But first, let me give you a little book by a man named Richard Foster. I like this guy. He is quite well known in certain circles and has written some fine books on spirituality. I've read a lot of his work. This little book, *Prayers from the Heart,* is one of my favorites. Perhaps you could take a look at this book and begin to try out some prayers of your own. We'll talk again tomorrow."

When she reached her room, Joan opened up the little book. She found a prayer called "Be the Gardener of My Soul." It was Joan's first prayer since her childhood. She didn't really know how to pray, but all her being was taken in by the words. She closed her eyes as a tear ran down her cheek.

Chapter 14
Friday: Prayer

Joan got up early enough to participate in matins. A little nervous, she took a book from a monk handing them out, and found her way to the third row—halfway down. Still a little sleepy, still a bit uncomfortable, she nonetheless felt a peace settle on her as she closed her eyes for the opening chants. She paid more attention to the words today, although the whole experience was still so new that complete understanding eluded her. She mostly allowed herself to savor the moment, which felt good and right. Today she wanted to talk to Brother Theodore about her own prayers from last night and resolved to find out what those stones were all about.

Brother Theodore was not at breakfast. Finishing her meal early she went outside to breathe in another warm, enchanting day in the desert. Tomorrow it would be over, and she felt sad. Yet she was looking forward to returning to work, to her home and her own bed and her Jacuzzi. It would be good to see Tracy again.

Wandering inside she made her way down the now-familiar hall. The door to Brother Theodore's office was open so she knocked lightly and walked in.

She sat down and began to speak even before he greeted her.

"Look, I've been thinking about what you've said, and especially about that piece from the Bible you quoted yesterday. And I'm troubled about one thing. Where does Jesus fit in all of this? I don't have to become a fundamentalist Christian, do I? I mean, you aren't fanatical. People here don't seem fanatical. They just seem deeply committed to a way of life. But in the outside world, it seems like people who talk about Jesus a lot are often strident, wear their religion on their sleeves, and are very reactionary both political and socially. I don't want to be like that."

Brother Theodore nodded. "No, Joan, you don't have to be like that. Take your friend Tracy, for example. Do you think she's a fanatic?"

"No, of course not."

"You see, there are Christians who are different from what you are talking about. People who take Jesus Christ seriously, who believe he is God without going around trying to change everyone and everything, who aren't as shrill as, say, some people in the Christian Right."

"Whew! That's a relief."

Brother Theodore smiled. "You'll begin to have other questions that relate to who Jesus is, but I'll answer those questions when you ask them."

"Okay. That's my first question. But it was a biggie. I'm sure I have a lot to learn about Jesus and God."

Brother Theodore smiled again. "Yes. And remember, Jesus is God."

"Oh."

Silence followed.

"Any more questions you'd like to ask?"

"Well, I'm sure there will be, after I leave. But right now I'm curious about those stones. When are you going to tell me what those stones are for, Brother Theodore?"

"Right now." The old man gave her a big smile and took something off the table. "Here's the first one."

On the newly polished stone someone had etched the word *prayer*. Brother Theodore then gave her a sheet of parchment on which was written in beautiful calligraphy a definition of prayer: *"Prayer is the interactive conversation between God and a person regarding what they are doing together."* Then Brother Theodore gave her back the small canvas bag in which she had collected her stones.

"You can keep this. I'll be sending you another stone every month for the next six months."

"Wow." Joan fondled the peach-colored stone and stroked the lettering, beautifully and carefully done. "What are the other stones going to be about?"

"Each will represent a different spiritual discipline. It will be accompanied by a description of the discipline. These disciplines have been practiced by serious Christians throughout the ages to attain a higher level of communion with God. But let's talk about this one on prayer. Did you look at the book last night?"

"Yes, I did. And I think I prayed, maybe for the first time in my life. I'm not yet sure that I believe in God. But I think I was praying as if I did. It was—odd."

"What do you think prayer is about, Joan?"

"Um, well, talking to a deity, a divine power, a god?"

"Sure, it's all of those, and more. The practice of prayer affirms a dimension to life that is unseen and immeasurable, while most human wisdom considers something important only if it is visible and quantifiable. The practice of prayer proclaims that people are spiritual beings, rooted in the heart, rather than only servants to an economic system, concerned primarily with personal net worth and an adequate retirement income. The practice of prayer invites God to be the watcher, guide, and protector of our lives, instead of being convinced that unless we stand up for ourselves, no one will."

Brother Theodore cocked an eye at Joan. "Look at it this way. We spend hours at the Y trying to hone our limited physical capabilities. Why not spend some concentrated effort strengthening our spiritual endowments?"

Joan smiled. It made good sense. Brother Theodore went on.

"Prayer is the unique opportunity that God gives us to develop a deeper understanding of him and of the world. It can anchor our lives by not only opening new vistas into the spiritual life, but also by tying us ever more firmly to God. You with me, Joan?"

"Sure. I think so." Joan marveled, thinking of her bland little Sunday school prayers as a child, mouthed but not felt.

"Let me give you an example of what I mean. One summer I spent a couple of months in San Francisco. The large office building in which I was consulting was next to a skyscraper construction site. It took the crew weeks just to drive the pilings deep into the ground. I still remember the earsplitting crashes of hammers, the rush of pressurized air, and the shouts of workers. They were anchoring the building, now among the tallest in San Francisco, deep into the bowels of the earth so not even a major earthquake would topple it. Prayer is like that. It anchors us to God by blasting through all our layers of debris and dirt so we might have a sturdy and strong life."

Joan had always been struck by the daring and ambition of big construction, and the comparison impressed her. "That would be some support to have," she said.

"It's available to you, Joan.

"In another book I like, *The Cloister Walk,* Protestant author Kathleen Norris writes about the ways the Catholic monastic tradition provides a rhythm and depth for spirituality. When she says that the life of prayer works 'the earth of the heart,' she means prayer is like the act of cultivation. In order to cultivate the soil, one must break up the hardened dirt clods, water the ground, free it from weeds, and then plant the crop. Prayer is the way to 'loosen up' the heart. During the natural course of our lives the 'earth of our heart' becomes parched, weed infested, and hard as flint. Unless we aerate and nourish that good soil in us, our lives become as destitute and dry as a wasteland."

When he finished, Joan sat silent for a while. "I would really like to be able to talk to God. But I'm not sure I even believe yet."

"That's okay. He's paying attention whether you believe or not. Now it's time for midday prayers. Why don't we meet again at 3:00? In the meantime maybe you can think a little more about prayer, perhaps write a prayer or two for yourself. Some words you can believe in."

"All right." And what on earth would those words be?

Joan spent the next forty-five minutes before lunch taking a walk. She would miss the desert. She walked down to the little spring that seemed a bit more shallow than it had been on Wednesday. Along the creek bed, she noticed more stones that would have worked for Brother Theodore's project and thought how charming ordinary stones could be if a person took the time to appreciate them.

When she arrived back at the refectory for lunch, she took a place in line behind Dianne. It was Dianne's last day, so after lunch they said good-bye. Suddenly Dianne reached out and surprised Joan with a big hug.

"Blessings to you, sister. Do take care, and don't stop growing."

"Thanks. I'm glad we met." Joan was a little embarrassed, but pleased too.

"So am I. Gotta run."

Joan watched Dianne leave. She'd only known the woman for a couple of days. Why did she feel so sad about her leaving?

When she met again with Brother Theodore, he talked to her more about Celtic prayer.

"You know, the Celtic Christians made prayer integral to every part of their lives. Esther De Waal, who has studied Celtic prayer, writes in one of her books about how weaving was second only to cooking as the activity that took up most of a Celtic woman's time. Women worked together because they couldn't handle the heavy looms by themselves. They only took time off from their many labors on the Sabbath, which started on Saturday evening and lasted until Monday morning. As women put up the loom for the weekend, they made the sign of the cross over it. Then they would pray for God's protection over every piece of machinery—the thrums, the pedals, the cogs and warp, the four posts, and so forth. They even included a prayer for the threads to prevent them from becoming tangled.

"Another chore many Celtic women tended to was milking their cows. Do you know they prayed over their thumb and each finger that milked the cow, and over each teat of the cow that was milked? Isn't that remarkable? I wonder how our lives would change if we prayed so meticulously over each part of our day, over each activity, over each chore, over each part of our bodies that performed those chores."

Brother Theodore made a plate of his empty hands. "Let me ask you a question, Joan. If I give you some exercises, a couple of things to do every day to help you grow in the discipline of prayer, would you be willing to commit yourself to them?"

Joan met the eyes of her friend. Yes—he had become that for her.

"I'd love for you to give me something concrete to do; I think it would help."

"Good. That tells me, Joan, that you are beginning to enter the fourth level of change—action. In putting your new insights and convictions into action you'll see yourself grow substantially. The concepts we've talked about this week cannot remain just nice ideas or nice stories. We must intentionally drive them deeper into our daily lives and consciousness in order for them to change us."

"So." Joan opened her hands into a receiving plate, too. "What shall I do?"

"Perhaps each morning you can begin your day with some simple prayers, one at a time, of course. What is your first activity of the day, Joan?"

Joan stifled a smirk but didn't want to say going to the bathroom, though there was probably a prayer for that. So she said, "Fixing my coffee."

"I thought that might be it. Remember Granné's prayer?'"

"Say it again for me."

"As I make this coffee to warm and waken our bodies, may the spirit of the Three descend on me to warm and waken my soul."

"That's so beautiful. Let me write it down." She took her small notebook out of her purse.

"Of course, there are lots of other possibilities. How do you get to work each day?"

"I usually take a commuter train."

"Okay, how could you pray about that daily ride?"

Joan winced. "Help me out. I'm not used to praying, Brother Theodore. Help me compose a couple of these."

"Okay. How about 'May the protection of the Three, Father, Son, and Holy Spirit, take me safely to my office.' It isn't fancy but it's a start."

"That sounds good to me."

"What else do you do each day?"

"Sometimes I see clients. Maybe I could just ask God to help me be a good listener, not to offend anyone."

"Good. I guess my first suggestion is simply to write some of those prayers down around each activity that you do every day. I assume you use a computer."

"Oh, yes. Impossible to be without one and succeed these days."

Brother Theodore smiled. "I could see you developing a prayer for your computer. Whatever all those pieces are, you know better than I. You could ask for protection over the printer, over the screen, over the various parts of the computer itself, over the electric current. You're a poet from way back, right? You could have fun with that one I'm sure."

Joan grimaced. "I don't know, Brother Theodore, that sounds a little over the edge."

He grinned. "Maybe. But not to the Celts. If they could pray over each teat of the cow they were milking, I'm sure they wouldn't think the parts of the computer would be too mundane to benefit from God's blessing. It would just be one way of making yourself open to God's grace and love throughout the course of each day.

"Here, Joan, is another book. Brother Lawrence was a monk who wrote letters to a certain individual—we don't have his name—who wanted to know about Brother Lawrence's prayer life. *Practicing the Presence of God* is the result of those letters. Brother Lawrence learned to experience the presence of God as he fulfilled his role in the monastery kitchen. He was consciously aware of God's presence as he washed each pot. I think the Celts would have approved.

"Before it gets too late in the evening, why don't you go and try to write something yourself?"

Joan spent the rest of the evening writing some prayers for everyday life. She giggled from time to time, a little giddy at the unfamiliar practice and wondering whether what she was writing was a little too silly for God, whom she'd always imagined as a serious fellow. *I guess not, if a Celtic woman could pray over a cow's teat.* She shook her head and giggled again, trying a prayer she wrote over the computer.

Bless the screen, bless the mouse, bless the hard drive, bless the hardware and the software.

Bless the electricity that gives energy.

Bless my mind and my hands as I guide these tools to productive ends.

That wasn't so hard. What else? It was so much fun that Joan didn't realize until quite late that she'd better call it a night.

Joan had been sleeping for only a couple of hours when she woke up to the sound of rain, gentle but steady. One of the rare rains in the desert. She got up and went to her window. She wondered whether it would be okay for her to go outside and walk in the rain. Already wearing her T-shirt, she pulled on her jeans and quietly left her room, tiptoed downstairs, stepped outside, and closed the door carefully behind her. The grainy sand tickled her bare feet, and the occasional sharp rock hurt, but she didn't care. The cool rain splashed her face, her hands, her feet. She began to dance and twirl. Not wanting to awaken anyone, she stifled to a whisper her ecstatic exclamation, "I'm alive! I'm alive!" *I sure hope no one is looking; they'll think I'm crazy.*

When she was thoroughly wet and a little chilly, she crept inside again, back to her room. She pulled her nightgown out of her suitcase, since now it was all she had to wear to bed. Just after she turned off the light, the sky flared white with lightning, a beautiful sky-to-earth streak. Her whole room was aflame for just an instant. Then it was dark again.

Going back to bed, Joan suddenly felt very alone. The deep darkness the lightning left was more dramatic than the lightning itself. Anxiety enveloped her, both about the week she had just experienced and about the week ahead when she would have to plunge back into the real world. She would not share this new piece of herself with her friends in the firm. Except for Tracy, of course, when they talked outside the office. She decided to go back and be the same Joan in the public eye. She would keep secret her new insights, the new glimmerings of faith that were like a growing seed inside.

Joan shuddered in her bed, not from cold but from fear, as the darkness became more oppressive. Would her colleagues see her differently when she returned? What did this week at the monastery have to do with her everyday life, after all? What would her colleagues say? Had she been a fool to come here? Was the change just an illusion that would disappear when she entered the real world again?

Until the wee hours of the morning she struggled, finally drifting unwillingly into a fitful sleep.

She had planned to go to matins again, but after last night she just couldn't pull herself out of bed. *Just thirty more minutes of sleep.* She reset her alarm. All too soon it jangled her awake. Then she dragged herself out of bed and went to the bathroom to splash cold water on her face. Was her dance in the rain a dream? After she took a quick shower and blew her hair dry, she stripped the linens off the bed. When she heard the sand brushed from her feet into the bed after her escapade fall onto the floor, she sighed in relief. The darkness had at least been preceded by something good and real. What in the world had last night been all about?

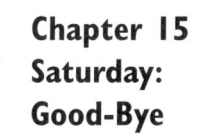

Chapter 15
Saturday:
Good-Bye

As planned, she went to Brother Theodore's office for breakfast. The door was open, and he was at the stove.

"Good morning, Joan. Your last day at the monastery. How does it feel?"

"A little sad. And I'm exhausted. I had a hard night."

"Oh, really? I'm sorry to hear that. Let's talk about it after we get started on breakfast."

He motioned her to the set table where a glass of fresh-squeezed orange juice awaited her. Brother Theodore sat down and asked if he could offer a prayer over the food.

"Certainly. I might as well get started on the first discipline."

"Oh, Lord, bless this food to our bodies and the conversation to the benefit of our souls, in the name of the Father, the Son, and the Holy Spirit. Amen." Joan saw that he crossed himself.

Then Brother Theodore poured her coffee; it even smelled better than what was served at the refectory. After she drank her orange juice he served her hot Irish oatmeal and fresh bran muffins with butter melted into them. Finally he spoke. "So, would you like to tell me about last night?"

"Well, I did something totally outlandish." She told him about her dance in the rain.

"That's not outlandish at all," Brother Theodore smiled. "That sounds perfectly delightful."

"What wasn't so delightful was what happened after I got in bed. There was this beautiful, bright display of lightning before I crawled into bed."

"I saw that, too. Magnificent."

"But it left such a darkness. And it seemed the darkness was folding itself around me, enveloping me. I began to wonder what this whole week here was all about. I decided that I was not going to let my colleagues, except Tracy, know anything about what I've experienced. I would go on as I always have, and keep this experience to myself."

"Why would you do that, Joan?" Brother Theodore did not sound accusing nor did Joan feel defensive about the question.

"Because I want to stay on good terms with everyone. I want to be respected. I don't want them to think that I've gone mushy or fanatical or something."

"That's interesting. May I suggest a possible motive behind that decision?"

"Sure."

"Perhaps it's pride that makes you want to retain your prestige and the respect of your colleagues."

"Is that bad?"

"Well, it's not healthy." He frowned ever so slightly. "It would be like smothering that wakening soul inside you. All the hard work you've done here at the monastery would be pushed aside. The light that has begun to shine in you would be extinguished. My strong impression is that you would like to keep growing. Am I right?"

"Yes, Brother Theodore. Of course. Though last night I was beginning to wonder whether I really did want to grow."

"You mean in the darkness?"

"Yes."

"Don't you think it's interesting that the darkness was preceded by that wonderful dance in the rain, where, it seems, your soul felt light and you were almost lifted up out of yourself?"

"That's a good description. Yes, I wondered why that happened that way."

"Joan you heard a beckoning from the dark side of who you are."

"I have a dark side?"

"Well, pride has always been considered one of the deadly sins, and it sounds to me like your pride was starting to crowd your light side, getting in the way of growth and enlightenment and spiritual health. We all have a dark side. And as human beings we will always struggle with it. Let me suggest a prayer you might try when you find yourself plagued by whatever dark influence you might be experiencing at any particular time. It's called the Jesus prayer. 'Lord Jesus Christ, Son of God, have mercy on me, a sinner.' Or something similar, like 'Lord have mercy, Lord have mercy, Lord have mercy.' That dark side of us is the part of us that rebels against God."

Joan ran a hand through her hair in exasperation. "But I thought Jesus was God. You just called him Son of God."

"Yes, Joan. It is very complex, and we can begin to unpack it in time. It's part of the doctrine of the Trinity, three persons, one God. Try not to get too hung up on that just now."

"Especially since I don't even know what I do believe. I'm willing to believe, even want to believe, but I'm not sure where I am in all that."

Brother Theodore smiled and squeezed Joan's arm in approval. "Your openness is very healthy. It's like an invitation to God to reveal more to you about who he is. One of my favorite prayers in the Bible came from a man who had asked Jesus to heal his ailing son. Jesus told him all things were possible if he believed. You know what the man said? 'Lord, I believe. Help my unbelief.' Then Jesus healed the son. (Mark 9:14 - 27) I still pray that prayer sometimes myself, when I'm in a difficult situation. God takes us where we are, Joan."

Joan felt hot tears well in her eyes again. "That is so beautiful."

"Well, time is getting away, unfortunately. Time is both a blessing and a curse. Perhaps it is our own busyness, what we try to stuff into time, that is the curse. Anyway, as usual I have to go soon. But I want to leave you with some parting words. I'd like you to consider beginning to build a spiritual library, starting with works on prayer. You are a very intelligent woman, but these are some new concepts for you. Start slow. I would suggest that you keep your prayer stone with you. When you need some comfort or a brief reminder of the monastery, hold it in your hand. It's not a magic charm, exactly, but I trust it will be an encouragement to you in your time of need, whatever the need is."

Brother Theodore rose and went to the window, bathed in morning light. "And nurture your soul by spending time outside. Nature walks. Or in the winter, perhaps go to a botanical garden. Or take more trips up to that cabin of yours. That sounds like a wonderful place for renewal. And finally, begin to spend time with other people of faith. Tracy is a great start. She can help you find others, I'm sure. You don't have to do anything wild or demanding. Just go to a show together, to a lecture, to the art museum at lunchtime. Those kinds of things. In just spending time with people of faith you can begin to develop your own."

Abruptly, he turned from the window, its brightness framing him. "Joan, have you been in touch with your office at all?"

"Before I went to bed last night, for the first time I called Tracy at home. We talked a little bit about prayer. But she wouldn't update me on stuff at the office—said there was nothing particularly urgent and it could wait till I got back."

Brother Theodore chuckled. "Good for Tracy. Hold on to that friend. Like I said, she's going to help you on this spiritual adventure. By the way, did you have time to create some prayers last night?"

"Yes. I brought them with me."

"Very good." He looked at the clock as a pained expression crossed his face. "Joan, I'm so sorry. I have really got to go; I'll be late for nones. Would you be willing to make copies for me? You can go down to the business office and tell them I'd like copies. They can put them in my box. I promise I'll read them and comment on them. I'm so sorry I can't look at them now."

Disappointed, Joan said politely, "That's okay. Sure, I'll have copies made."

Brother Theodore reached for a notebook on a shelf and leafed through it. Pulling out a page he said, a little shyly, Joan thought, "Here is a poem I wrote myself. Get a copy of this at the office, too, and take it with you. I think it addresses the issue of light and darkness we just talked about."

The chimes for nones began to sound.

"One more thing, Joan. Don't expect too much of yourself. You've had a dislocating experience. You've been dropped into a different world from the one you are used to. So it will take a day or two at least to hit your stride at work."

Brother Theodore gave Joan a big hug, and Joan noticed tears in his eyes. "I'm going to miss you, friend. It's been a great blessing to me for you to be here. It's always very special to participate in the spiritual awakening of another human being. You know where to write to me if you'd like to ask any questions or share any insights. I'd love to hear from you. And I will be sending you those last six stones over the course of the next several months." He took a small vase with a coral-colored rose in it from a shelf. "This is a Granné rose. It may not last long on your flight and everything, but enjoy it while you can."

He encouraged Joan out the door and closed it behind him. "Blessings, sister." And he was off toward the oratory. As he hurried away—he was late today, and that was unusual for Brother Theodore, she knew—emotion welled up in her throat. She took a deep breath and swallowed. Then she read his poem.

The Power of Light

I sit and see the power that brings the sunrise
My spirit is overcome by it
Where there is darkness, light overcomes
The light is the power that each beam brings
That leads to the path of insight
I see and know the power behind the sunrise
I sit and feel that power that brings the sunrise
My spirit is at one with the sunrise
I see this power . . .
It brings light to day
Each beam leads to a path of insight

A ragged sigh escaped from her depths.

When she completed her errand in the business office and made sure everything was ready to go, Joan took one last walk, heading for the little stream. A warm breeze caressed her face, and her eyes squinted against the sun. *What is it like in Chicago today? I guess I'll find out soon enough.* Even apart from the weather, which was bound to be cold, a sharp contrast to this serene place awaited her at home. She tried to imprint these scenes and sensations in her mind. She remembered the story of the little village and how dark it had been before the monk came. And how the people of the village thought their life was normal until the monk showed them what normal was. She felt like she had caught a glimpse of normal and wanted her life to be more like that. She thought about the darkness of the night before. In contrast, she felt very peaceful in this light of day, washed clean by the night rain.

She would miss Brother Theodore. She would like to attend more of the prayer services. She wished she could absorb more of the quiet, put it in a bottle to open and savor when things at work got frenetic. How could she develop a rhythm for her own life that would help her along her way? She still had so much internal clutter to deal with. Holding the prayer stone in her hand reminded her of one way she could get past clutter.

She wandered down to the little creek and saw that the rain had engorged it. How deep was it now? Joan couldn't help herself. She took off her shoes and went wading once again. This time the creek was almost ankle deep. And colder than before because the sun had not yet warmed it. Checking her watch again, almost angrily she realized it was time to leave.

Joan reached the airport with plenty of time to spare. In a gift shop she found a two-pound bag of plump Hawaiian macadamia nuts for Tracy and a box of Ghiradelli chocolates for Margaret. For Chip she bought a new Swiss army knife. For Alison, food wouldn't work. But she would enjoy a book on the desert's flora and fauna. Alison the literary scholar was also the nature lover of the family. And for Brad she bought a book on ancient Asian mummies.

On arriving at O'Hare, she immediately connected with an airport limousine and arrived home by 4:00 Chicago time.

When the limousine arrived at her doorstep, she got out, saw her breath in the chill air, and walked slowly up the steps to her front door. She took in the patches of snow, the leafless trees and shrubs, the gray-brown gloom of winter in Chicago. *Home again. I was so anxious to get here. Now I'm here and I really want to go back.* She opened the door lethargically and stepped up into the entryway. She wondered whether Chip was around, but everything was quiet. Except for a couple of things tossed on chairs, she wasn't sure whether he'd even been around. After she hung up her coat, she checked around to see whether he was in, but no sign of Chip. She checked her answering machine. Seventeen messages, ugh. Well, they had waited this long, they could wait a couple more hours.

Suddenly Joan shook herself. *Get with it. Enough of this loathsome self-pity. What would be a good pick-me-up?* Even before the question formed itself she knew the answer. *Time for some jazz, a White Russian, a few candles, and the Jacuzzi.* Immediately energized she began the bath, then went to the kitchen, pulled out the milk, and checked it for freshness—good, Chip must have gotten some groceries. She mixed her drink, set up the stereo—mostly jazz, including John Coltrane's album with "You Don't Know What Love Is." After undressing, lighting the candles, and adding aromatherapy crystals to the bath, she lowered herself into wonderful, warm water and began to soak.

After drying and pulling her terry robe around her, instead of looking at her things from the monastery—there would be plenty of time for that—she climbed into bed. It was good to be back in her own bed. And the darkness tonight, Joan noted as she turned off the light, was not fearful at all. It enveloped her in great comfort. Soon she fell into a deep, peaceful sleep. She didn't even hear Chip come home and check in on her or see the smile on his face at being assured that his mom had arrived home safely from wherever.

Joan started awake. Where was she? Where were the chants; didn't they sing on Sunday? Then she smiled. *Home. I'm back home. In my own bed again. In my own house.* She was surprised at how happy that made her. She checked the time: 7:15. She quickly went downstairs to fix some coffee, remembering Granné's coffee prayer. "As I fix this coffee to warm and waken my body, Spirit of the Three, descend on me, to warm and waken my soul." She crossed herself. *Am I doing this right? Decent coffee at last.* It was probably the thing she had missed most at the monastery. After the coffee began to brew, she put on more music; this time she opted for symphonies and some piano concertos. Just then Chip appeared at the top of the stairs, hair a mess, pajamas askew.

"Hi, Mom. Good to have you back." He came over and gave her a bear hug. "I missed you. Did you get religion?"

He didn't smell great—obviously hadn't taken his shower and certainly hadn't brushed his teeth—but he looked wonderful to her.

"I don't know that I'd say I got religion, buddy, but I got some peace and quiet, that's for sure. It's good to see you, too. What a nice surprise. I thought you'd still be at Dad's."

"He dropped me off about 8:00 last night because he and Gina had a late dinner engagement, and he thought someone should be here to welcome you home. Only you were already out like a light."

"How was your week?"

"Good. Do you want to make me breakfast or shall I fix breakfast for you?"

"Tell you what. You go get showered and dressed, and I'll fix us breakfast. Is there any food in the house?"

"Sure, I just picked up some things yesterday. I see you found the milk. Have a White Russian first thing when you got home? No alcohol at the monastery?"

"They had wine, but no White Russians. Thanks for getting the milk. It really hit the spot yesterday."

"Tell me all about it at breakfast."

This was nice. She'd expected to be alone today. It was going to be good to have someone else around. And he certainly seemed upbeat. *I wonder what's up?*

Sundays at the monastery were different from other days. There was regular church, with the celebration of the Eucharist. Breakfast before and lunch after were much smaller, since people from the previous week had mostly left, and people for the next week usually arrived late Sunday or on Monday. So it was quieter than usual. Brother Theodore was acutely aware of Joan's absence today. He was sure he would see her again, but he would miss their daily meetings, miss seeing her grow, her face alight at a new concept. It was lonely today. And he was tired. He would wait it out, allow all the feelings of grief, loneliness, and fatigue to take their turns. For these, he knew, were also part of the rhythms of life.

Letter One

Joan unwrapped the carefully wrapped package. Inside was a letter along with a piece of parchment around something small and hard. She untied and opened the bundle, and out fell one of her smooth stones with the word *study* written on it. This parchment also had a definition written on it:

Chapter 16
Letters

STUDY
(as a spiritual discipline)
Intentional process whereby the mind takes in new information, then accommodates it with its own worldview and allows the information to extend and modify that worldview.

She opened the letter.

Dear Joan,

Can you believe it's been a month since you left the monastery? Or maybe it seems a lifetime ago to you. I received your letter more than a week ago now. I would have answered sooner, but I knew I would be sending this next stone, so I decided to send them together.

Of course, Joan, you know about study, having been to college and law school. As a lawyer you know how to accumulate information and store it for future use. But this kind of study is an active spiritual exercise that affects the way you think, feel, and act, when it is accommodated into your life as well as your mind.

Before we study, we don't always know the right questions. Study helps us define our questions and form new ones. Your study will begin to produce images that are concrete concepts, much as Michelangelo would discover an image emerging as he sculpted.

I hope this is helpful as you read and ponder. Well, enough on study for now. Now to your letter.

I'm glad you went to church with Tracy. It's okay that it didn't really suit you. Ethnic and cultural differences are not bad things, and it sounds like that's what you are talking about. You will probably want to experiment some more. There are many Christian churches that proclaim God's truth, and each has a somewhat different emphasis; I would have to say, though, that some more completely offer God's message than others. I will be happy to guide you as you look around for a place of worship, if you like.

It is interesting that Margaret has begun to ask you more about your experience, especially after the initial teasing you wrote about. It sounds like life has been heavy for her, with a developmentally disabled son, and now she is experiencing some health problems of her own. It's good that you want to stand by her as she tries to give up smoking. It's a struggle you have overcome, and you know how hard it is. Be gentle with her. Her hard edges were created by the storms she's weathered in life. It sounds like she has taken her pain and walked away from God, as I did. You and Tracy together are well placed to help her find her way back.

I will always be pleased to hear from you and will always write back in what I hope is a timely fashion.

Peace and blessings to you, dear sister Joan.

Brother Theodore

Letter Two

MEDITATION

Synthesizing information, sounds, sights, senses, and ideas, and opening all of these to God, so God may work in your life to mold your worldview and image of God.

Dear Joan:

It was good to hear from you again. I will answer your letter in due course. First, let me talk about the next spiritual discipline, which, if you have looked at the new stone, you already know is meditation.

Meditation is the process of pondering information stored in the brain by study. Through meditation you will begin to accommodate information into your worldview in a way that will reshape your image of God. Study and meditation work together to extend your spiritual boundaries, reforming your perspective into something new and mature. Study and meditation begin to build resources that help you develop rhythm, harmony, and balance, just as Tracy said.

Regarding meditation, I've been thinking over your last letter. I would encourage you not to just get caught up in the tumble of ideas from your mind. Put soul development first. Even as you think about what you are learning, be aware of breathing, stillness, body sensations, and the riches of silence. This is not thought control as in legal briefs. It is allowing thoughts to meander across the field. Where your mind takes you, don't hesitate to follow, but don't get stuck there. Allow yourself the joy of being aware of what is happening with your breath. The breath of God as it gives you life.

Remember the garden at the monastery where you liked to rest and think things through? The place you forced yourself to return to after running away from the unpleasant feelings that crept up on you? When you meditate, got your body and emotions ready by reminiscing about that garden. Pretend you are there. Allow your body to remember the sensations of sitting on the stone bench, the breath of the wind against your face, the warmth of the sun, the gurgling of the fountain, the peal of the chimes calling for prayer. Remember the butterfly that met you in the garden when you returned from your panic that afternoon? Think of yourself as a beautiful butterfly emerging from a cocoon.

Grist for your meditation can be, but should not be limited to, the new ideas you are gleaning from your study, the new concepts and thoughts. Those are worth pondering. But meditation is not just about words or ideas or rational concepts. You can meditate on a flower—perhaps the first tulips or daffodils that find their way above the earth in the first weeks of spring. Perhaps the little squirrel that stops and stares at you when you are picking dandelions out of your yard. Meditation includes concentrating on the senses that come to you from nature—enjoying them, feeling them. These thoughts, sensations, and images can all work together with the cognitive part of you to help you achieve the rhythm, harmony, and balance you seek in your life.

Of course, Joan, meditation can occur throughout your day. Most people don't have time to carve out large pieces of their day simply to meditate. It's important to dedicate some of your time to meditation, of course. But you can meditate on the way to work. If you have your stones on your desk at work, when you look at them you can briefly be aware of them, what they mean, or simply recall the fact that the disciplines are becoming part of your life.

This is probably a good time to point out that these spiritual disciplines overlap each other. Meditation relates to study when you are reflecting on a new idea and trying to figure out how you can implement a new activity into your life. And meditation will connect with the other disciplines as well. They are all part of a tapestry of spirituality that we can, with God's help, weave into our lives.

Now to your letter.

I was pleased that Tracy and a couple of your other friends went for makeovers. You have always looked fine to me, but we can see this as another outward demonstration of something happening inside. The choice to make some outer changes that will make you feel good about yourself reminds me of that butterfly I mentioned. I'm not too up on fashion or makeup, but I know that women like experimenting with them. Some women have told me that reaching fifty frees them to be who they are in every aspect of their being. Instead of being held hostage to current fashions and trends, they find what is right for them. Through the years of changing fashions, they have discovered what most becomes them and what works with their own lifestyle. You are not quite fifty, I know. But think in terms of becoming your own person, in every aspect of your life. Not being tossed around by every new idea or trend that blows your way. That goes for intellectual and spiritual trends as well.

I'm glad to hear that Tracy has helped you find a small group of people who are interested in developing some sense of community outside of work. I told you there are probably more legal types like you and Tracy who want more in life than their professions. Going to the Art Institute on a Saturday sounded really good. Good to get out of the house. Good to do something different. Good to contemplate great art. Restoration for the soul.

The jazz club sounds like fun, too. Hope you can find time to do more of that kind of thing. It really is true that all work and no play makes us rather dull, not just to be around, but dull in our spirits. It is also true that we were intended to live life with others. I'm glad you are finding others to share life with.

Well, dear sister, the chimes are ringing for vespers. One day I hope you will return to worship and pray with us. Until next month.

Brother Theodore

Letter Three

SIMPLICITY

An inward reality that results in a changed outward lifestyle.

Dear Joan,

Another month has passed already. Is April a pretty time in Chicago? I imagine leaves emerging on your trees and flowers beginning to bloom. Is there more sunshine in Chicago these days? I'm sure it is progressing to warmer weather in spite of the late snowstorm you mentioned in your last letter. Ah, snow. I have to go to the mountains to see it here. I think I got my fill of the stuff when I lived in France and Massachusetts. The movement of the seasons from winter to spring reminds us of the hope we can have in God to give new life.

If you've looked at your new stone, you'll know that the spiritual discipline for this month is simplicity.

What is simplicity? Well, try this. I love a quote from the *Tao Te Ching* that says: "Be content in what you have. Rejoice in the way things are. When you realize there is nothing lacking, the whole world belongs to you." That's a pretty good definition of simplicity.

Simplicity touches on control of our minds, our bodies, our souls, our emotions. Godly people try to battle pride, gluttony, and laziness. I'm sure you are aware that in this country we consume a lion's share of the world's resources. It is entirely questionable whether what we contribute makes up for what we consume.

As individuals, we can counter the common way of our world and try to consume less. Less food. Less energy. Less "stuff." In return for taking in less, we paradoxically have more to give to others. We are less focused on ourselves, on our material accumulation, so we have more resources to share. We eat less and have more energy for service (another discipline we will talk about in time). In consuming less electrical and less fossil fuel energy, we find ourselves getting more exercise, going out less, and having more time for contemplation, saving time by doing our errands in one trip. If we do these things as ends in themselves, they can become drudgery. But when we use this discipline of simplicity to energize and expand our ability to nurture our souls and reach out to nurture others, they become a means toward the holy end of spiritual development.

You may have seen the little volume *Simplify Your Life: 100 Way To Slow Down and Enjoy the Things That Really Matter* by Elaine St. James. Here are some of her suggestions:

> Take off your shoes and enjoy the feel of the carpet or grass on your feet.
>
> Have a simple cup of tea and sit down in a comfortable chair to savor it.
>
> While lighting the fire, feel the texture of the wood, smell deeply the aroma of newly lit logs, enjoy the colors of the fire, the sounds of it consuming the wood.
>
> When going for a walk, concentrate on the colors and sounds of nature, and the breeze kissing your cheek.
>
> When communicating with friends, write letters and post them, instead of always depending on e-mail. Take time to enjoy forming the letters with your hand, watching the ink as it bleeds across the paper. Be aware of the texture of the paper and the sound of the pen as it makes its way across the page.
>
> While listening to music, turn off the phone.

After a busy day, when you arrive home sit down for five or ten minutes, close your eyes, think of something good, and allow that contemplation to refresh you, to give you pleasure. And remember to include in your discipline of simplicity a constant attitude of thankfulness to God for the good things in your life: friends, food, clothing, heat in winter and cool air in summer, family, shelter.

Let me remind you again that all of these disciplines are interconnected, part of a tapestry of the soul.

Brother Theodore

Letter Four

SOLITUDE

Creation of space in which we can be found by God and by which we are freed from competing loyalties.

Dear Joan,

I'm glad to hear that the weather has taken a turn for the better in Chicago. Good for you for taking time to enjoy those crocuses and the daffodils and tulips. The lilac park in the suburbs you mentioned sounds absolutely heavenly. You are coming along in your journey to a deeper spiritual self.

As you now know, this month's discipline is solitude. Solitude doesn't just happen in a completely empty room, though spending time in one can contribute to solitude of the heart. Spiritual solitude is, rather, a space in the heart made clean for God's presence. It is about being internally silent. It reminds me a bit of dropping a pebble into a pond and watching the ripples rush to the edges, and then waiting for the surface to grow quiet.

Solitude is about seeing the dark as well as the light side of yourself. You experienced that dramatically at the monastery. It is seeking out an internal place away from both internal and external clutter. Solitude is one of the most difficult disciplines. It requires a real commitment to the quiet side of life. It does not necessarily demand aloneness, but it does require a recognition that you are alone. The collection of stones you now have can help you meditate as well as help take you to the quiet inner place.

Rather than thinking of solitude as literal aloneness or silence, think of it as a static-free zone. A place where you can think, doze—a place for holy leisure, the kind that truly replenishes the soul.

In developing the discipline of solitude, remember some of the principles of relaxation.

1. Literal, external quiet, as much as possible.
2. Decreased muscle tension.
3. A mental device to help you reach that quiet inner place, like holding one of the stones in your hand, concentrating both on the word on the stone and on the feel of the stone in your hand. (I was interested to hear you say that you sometimes feel heat in your hand when you hold one of the stones.)
4. A passive attitude. Don't try to control the free floating of ideas.

Solitude is not an exercise to be experienced. It is a discipline that allows God to mediate grace to us. Pray for the grace of solitude, the gift of meditation, the soul's work of study. You are slowly being molded into a more perfect image of God.

Inner solitude and silence are necessary because your mind will never stop trying to fix problems. Capture your mind and focus it in meditation and solitude. (Our disciplines are overlapping again!)

So some of your colleagues are asking about the stones on your desk? Your response is a healthy one: "Yes, they remind me of some things I learned at the monastery, and which I continue to learn." You're right that you have no reason to feel defensive, and no real reason to go into any extended explanation unless your friends ask more about it. And some will, in time, especially as it become more and more apparent that you are changing.

Your letters are a great encouragement to me because they demonstrate that you truly are changing and growing. You continually find new ways of putting the disciplines into practice. You haven't forgotten. You are working at it. If there is one further piece of encouragement I would give you, it is, "Remember the process."

It has been a busy couple of weeks here at the monastery with some novices preparing for entry to the order. It so refreshing to work with new men. I wish I had more life to give. But as for all of us, life is short, it runs out, and we must all take stock of whether our activities have been worthwhile, whether our lives are being or have been well spent. It's not just at middle age that you ask these questions. I ponder them every day during my personal prayers. And I pray for God's grace to allow me, like St. Paul, to forget (and forgive) what is behind, and to reach forward to what lies ahead. (Philippians 3:13, New King James Version)

Enough meandering for now. And remember the process.

Brother Theodore

Letter Five

SERVICE
Experiencing the many little deaths of going beyond ourselves, which produces in us the virtue of humility.

Dear Joan:

Your last letter arrived just yesterday. I decided to send the service stone a few days early so I could encourage you by addressing your issues, affirm your new relationship, and encourage you in this new discipline. Sort of a three-pronged purpose.

I know what you mean about solitude being very hard to cultivate. Keep in mind that you are probably experiencing it to some degree as you study and as you meditate. Our culture doesn't make real solitude easy. It's hard to be quiet without having our busy minds intrude. In your case, arguing cases, defending clients, engaging with family members, and remembering your own mistakes will vie for your attention. These emotional weights are the clutter that continues to fight the place of calm at your center.

Let me give you a little example of what it's like. Say there is a deep well and a quiet, isolated place that is very hard to get to because all around it is growth, and stones, and debris. Each time you go to that quiet, isolated place, you have to hack away at the path to get through. But if you do it regularly, eventually the path becomes more clear, the debris stays away longer, the plants take longer to grow back.

This is like the soul—your center.

I am delighted to hear about your new relationship with the Greek Orthodox man. You must think he is very handsome indeed if he looks like a fifty-year-old JFK, Jr. When you write of your experience in his church, it seems similar to your response to Tracy's church. It is a great cultural change from anything you have experienced. You have the added incentive of a romantic interest to try to make it work, but please go slowly. Give yourself time to adjust.

It's interesting that the music sounds like music from heaven. The Orthodox really do work hard to experience a little bit of the Kingdom of Heaven during liturgy. In fact, it's another kind of spiritual discipline. I'm glad you are comfortable with the incense. It could have been different given your experience at your grandfather's funeral all those years ago.

For what it is worth, I encourage this new interest in David, and I'm glad you are open again to love in your life. Just don't take any of it too fast. I'm glad he is committed to his faith and is helping you understand and is not pushing you in the relationship. He sounds like a good friend, first and foremost.

Interestingly, Joan, your discussion of his pro bono work for Tracy's South Side Center and the interest you have in reaching out and helping those less fortunate than yourself is a true mark that you are growing in spirit and faith.

Service is an important spiritual discipline, one that puts feet on what is going on inside us. St. James tells us that faith without works is a dead thing (James 2:17). Service then, as mentioned in the parchment description, is experiencing the many little deaths of going beyond ourselves, which produces in us the virtue of humility.

What does that mean? It simply means that looking outside ourselves to those in need, and offering assistance where we are able, allows us to humble ourselves to participate in their need. Service as a spiritual discipline is not just the haves giving to the have-nots. It is thankfully and humbly sharing what we have and do not need with those who have not and deserve as much as we do. Make sense? Mull it over.

I know, Joan, that you have to put so many billable hours into your practice to retain your partnership. Those are the rules, and we are all regulated by some kind of rule in our place of employment. I am not suggesting that you give up your hard-won time with your friends or your time for personal study and meditation. I am suggesting that you add to and balance these with some kind of service. It doesn't have to be on David's level. He sounds like he may have more time available at this juncture in his life. In fact, your service does not have to be legal advice. Do people in David's church serve at a homeless shelter once a month? That could be your service for now. Does your company have a childcare center? You could volunteer there an hour a week or a month. Any activities that remind you of your humanity and dependence, most of all, on the goodness and grace of God for every breath of life. I think you get the idea.

Joan, I can hardly wait to send you the final stone. Has it really been five months since you were here? The final stone will have a lighter feel, I think. Until then.

Brother Theodore

Letter Six

CELEBRATION

A life of experiencing moments of grace and being thankful.

Dear Joan,

Here is the last stone that you found at the monastery stream six months ago. I'm so pleased to be able to give this to you, knowing how diligently you are applying yourself to the other disciplines. This discipline should bring you great pleasure, and hopefully will be easier than some.

While celebration does not necessarily mean throwing a big party, and certainly does not connote getting plastered on a Friday night, it might include occasionally throwing a party for friends to acknowledge some good gift of God—friendship, a successful legal effort. In fact, as you mentioned Chip and his reacceptance into law school, I thought it was particularly appropriate that you celebrated with him when you fixed his favorite dinner, then gave thanks to God for you both before you ate. Then you celebrated with your friends who had been praying with you about Chip's status in the school. It's important for some of our celebration to be with the community that assists us in our spiritual adventure.

But most of the time celebration isn't a big production. It should be part of every day. Celebration is simply being aware of the good things in life, acknowledging a loving God who gives those things to you, and allowing those moments and experiences to grace your lives and strengthen you to go on. The first flower of spring, the rainbow after a storm, the fragrance of newly turned earth, the cold drink after a warm and harried day. Consciously allowing these simple pleasures to impress themselves on you many times each day and receiving them gratefully from the hand of a loving God will begin to impact your life in a way that will become noticeable to those who know you. They will see the grace that comes from your life toward them and toward your clients.

I agree with you that David is a great gift of grace to you. I'm glad he is so supportive of you. And I'm glad he is sharing his own family with you; his grandchildren sound lovely. Maybe here is a chance to address some of those things about your past that you regret. Maybe this is a chance to be a better mother, so to speak. Most people probably get it better the second time around as grandparents. But you are also giving something to David's children as you love and care for their children. The ability to love other people's kids is a great gift to them.

When you hold that new baby, you can accept that warm bundle in your arms as a gift of grace to you. When you help little Georgie to climb on the jungle gym, the satisfaction you receive is a gift of grace. Be thankful for all those kinds of things. Enjoying the little things in life is celebration. And all the celebration adds grace to how you live your life.

Joan, you have come so far since I first met you, not quite a year ago. I have been so blessed to be a part of your life formation. I hope that our communication does not end here. Please always feel free to contact me, to ask any questions or share any experience. I would love for you to keep me posted about your relationship with David.

As always, you are and continue to be in my prayers.

Peace and blessing, dear sister Joan. Keep growing.

Brother Theodore

Epilogue

The hot apricot tea warmed her hands as she held the cup, and then her insides as she sipped it tentatively at first, then in gulps as it quickly cooled in the night air. It was a Friday night in late September. Joan Alexander rubbed the back of her neck, then put her head back on the Adirondack chair. Though it had been a sticky-warm day in Chicago, up here fall was quickly approaching with its chill, dry air.

It felt so good to be out of her work clothes. As she was doing more and more on weekends, she'd left her work at the office. She only had her cell phone, in case any of her family needed her. She wasn't as sleepy as she thought she should be and had come out to the porch to wind down, to inhale the quiet for a while. And it was quiet. Quiet and dark. No lights, only the stars. No sirens, no phone, no stereo. She heard only a distant owl and the deep night silence

As she sat under the stars, Joan's thoughts drifted to the events of the past year—the weekend she had spent with Margaret and Tracy, the weekend that had really started it all, the week at the monastery, and all the ordinary times since then that also had begun to change her.

She had come up here this evening by herself to think, to meditate, and to review. It was sort of a way to celebrate, as Brother Theodore had said. She would have solitude, she would pray, she would meditate, maybe she would study, though there was plenty of information stored in her brain to keep her busy for quite some time.

Mostly she needed to review the past year and a half and celebrate all the good things that had happened in her life. Not least of these was her relationship with David. And the easy simplicity of this place.

This was not a night of sorrow and remorse. This was a night and a weekend to be thankful. And to contemplate the future.

She had one of her stones with her—celebration. As she held it now it warmed her hand. It was not the intense heat that these stones sometimes emitted. The heat emanating from the rock tonight was her own heat, which the rock was returning to her. Sort of like the moon beaming back the light given it by the sun.

She also needed to consider her future in the firm, which wanted so much of her life. She didn't know anymore whether it was what she still chose. She had recently been looking at small condos in the city to save money and to be closer to work. And also to be closer to the South Side Center, where she and David spent much of their spare time giving legal help to people who needed it but could not pay the market prices for good lawyers. She had learned to call it *pro deo* instead of pro bono. It was not just for good, it was to the glory of God. That made it feel even more important. It wasn't just passing off your extra time to the poor. It was making that effort an offering to God, and she felt more incentive to really do her best, to treat each client as very important in their own right. She had read that

Mother Theresa had tried to see the face of Christ in the face of each person who came into her refuge in India.

For the first time in her life, Joan was beginning to feel the limitations of her own energy. As long as she didn't divide it, as long as it all went to the firm, she hadn't noticed any shortage. But now that she was trying to divide herself between the requirements of her profession and her spiritual activities, she discovered that her personal resources were indeed limited. And she no longer wanted to give it all to the firm. She wanted time for David. And Tracy. And her lunch group. And her kids. She'd even like to do a little traveling. She wanted to visit Greece with David, whose grandparents had lived and died there. He had shared with her his interest in the Balkans and his wish to do something positive for that part of the world.

But tonight, she was putting it all on hold. She simply wanted to enjoy the night sky, the brilliance of the stars, the half-moon shining above her. She had come to believe that the Creator of all these did indeed care about the creation he had flung into being. And this Creator cared about her. She knew it now. It had been shown to her in a hundred different ways, through Tracy, through Brother Theodore, through David. Through the many graces she had observed in her family's life— Chip who had reentered law school with a new attitude; Charles with whom she had become friends again; her daughter who had begun to share her studies and her new social life with her mother (she should add England to her list of places to travel); Brad who had embarked on his own spiritual journey at the university and was excited about his mother's new spiritual insights.

For all of these she was deeply thankful to the God who cared.

As the stars shined brighter, she caught a glimpse of something she had only been lucky enough to see two or three times in her life—the aurora borealis. The blues and greens and magentas began to intensify and dance in the sky. She was suddenly caught up in the dance, standing and raising her arms and moving her feet and humming. *What is it they always say at David's church? Glory to thee, oh our God, glory to thee.*

Works Cited

pp. 37 New King James Version, Thomas Nelson Publishers (Nashville, 1983, Thomas Nelson, Inc.)

pp. 40 Quoted in Harry R. Moody, Ph.D., and David Carroll, *Five Stages of the Soul*. (New York: Anchor Books, 1997), p. 2.

pp. 130 Eugene N. Peterson, *The Message: The New Testament in Contemporary English* (Colorado Springs, CO: NavPress Publishing Group, 1993).

pp. 131 Richard J. Foster, *Prayers from the Heart*. (New York: Harper Collins, 1993), p. 3.

pp. 137 Kathleen Norris, *The Cloister Walk*. (New York: Riverhead Books, 1996).

pp. 138 Esther De Waal, *The Celtic Way of Prayer: The Recovery of the Religious Imagination* (New York: Image Books, 1997), p. 80, 81, 84–86.

pp. 141 Brother Lawrence, *The Practice of the Presence of God with Spiritual Maxims*. (Grand Rapids, MI: Fleming H. Revell, 1999).

pp. 162 Quoted in Joan Chittister, *The Rule of Benedict: Insights for the Ages*. (New York: The Crossroad Publishing Company, 1992), p. 52.

pp. 163 Elaine St. James, *Simplify Your Life: 100 Ways to Slow Down and Enjoy the Things That Really Matter*. (New York: Hyperion, 1994).

About the Author

Glandion Carney is the author of five books, a leader in the Renovare Movement, founded by Richard J. Foster, and is chaplain for the Christian Legal Society. He lives in Birmingham, Alabama.

> *"...the language of the wise brings healing."*
> Proverbs 12:18b

About the Press

At PageMill Press, we publish books that explore and celebrate the Christian life. Our titles cover a wide range of topics, including spiritual memoir, devotional and contemplative life, peace and justice, faith-based community work, spiritual disciplines, reference works, family and parenting, spirituality, and fiction.

We believe that publishing involves a partnership between the author, publisher, bookseller, and reader. Our commitment as a publisher to this partnership is to produce wise and accessible books for thoughtful seekers across the full spectrum of the Christian tradition.

The Press seeks to honor the writer's craft by nurturing the felicitous use of language and the creative expression of ideas. We hope and believe that knowledge and wisdom will result.

For a catalogue of PageMill Press publications, for editorial submissions, or for queries to the author, please direct correspondence to: PageMill Press, 2716 Ninth Street, Berkeley, CA 94710; Ph. 510-848-3600; Fax 510-848-1326.

MORE PAGEMILL PRESS TITLES

FAITH WORKS: HOW FAITH-BASED ORGANIZATIONS ARE CHANGING LIVES, NEIGHBORHOODS AND AMERICA
A genre-busting book that includes elements of personal memoir, spiritual vision, social strategy, politics, and theology.
Jim Wallis / Foreword by Bill Moyers
$16.95 ISBN 1-879290-23-5

THE BOY WHO CRIED ABBA: A PARABLE OF TRUST AND ACCEPTANCE
A charming and compelling retelling of the gospel story through the eyes of an orphaned and disabled child.
Brennan Manning / Foreword by Amy Grant
$13.95 ISBN 1-879290-7

THINKING WITH THE HEART: A MONK (AND PARENT) EXPLORES HIS CHRISTIAN HERITAGE
A beautifully written exploration of the author's Christian legacy and a spiritual will and testament for all seekers.
Tolbert McCarroll
$13.95 ISBN 1-879290-21-9

EVERYONE WANTS TO GO TO HEAVEN BUT…WIT, FAITH, AND A LIGHT LUNCH
An ABC of terms that helps the reader turn Christianity upside down and inside out and in the process actually helps us find new ways to look at faith.
C. McNair Wilson / Foreword by Ken Davis
$14.95 ISBN 1-879290-16-2

FINDING FAITH: LIFE-CHANGING ENCOUNTERS WITH CHRIST
The author tells the stories of people who in ways both expected and unexpected have come to faith and are willing to talk about their doubts and joys.
Sharon Gallagher
$13.95 ISBN 1-879290-17-0

REAWAKENING TO LIFE: RENEWAL AFTER A HUSBAND'S DEATH
Remarkable stories of how ordinary women make the transition from widowhood to seeing themselves as new people.
Mary Ellen Berry
$13.95 ISBN 1-879290-24-3